What's in a name?

The origins of station names on
the London Underground
and Docklands Light Rail

Cyril M. Harris

Published in co-operation with the
London Transport Museum

CAPITAL HISTORY

ISBN 185414 241 0

Published by
Capital History,
www.capitalhistory.com

Designed by Tim Demuth

Printed in the EU

Photographic credits

Capital Transport collection:
    pages 6, 13, 17, 19, 31, 36, 40, 43, 50, 51
    52, 54, 56, 63, 74.

Tim Demuth:
    pages 2, 7, 10, 15, 20, 21, 22, 23, 25, 26,
    32, 45, 47, 50, 65, 67, 71, 72, 78, 82.

LT Museum:
    pages 9, 11, 27, 29, 34, 37, 42, 46, 48, 57,
    58, 62, 66, 68, 72, 75, 77, 81.

Mike Seaborne:
    page 14.

This was the second arch to be constructed over Archway Road and was opened in 1813. The original arch was a 300m tunnel along this deviation of the Great North Road, which had been built to avoid the steep Highgate Hill. It opened towards the end of 1809, but collapsed in 1812. The present iron bridge replaced the arch illustrated in 1897.

Introduction

Like many Londoners I sit (or stand) most days on a London Underground train and, besides reading my newspaper, look at the maps and signs displaying the routes of the different lines and wonder how the stations obtained their names. Why is Leicester Square so named when it is so far from Leicester? Why is Tottenham Court Road many miles away from Tottenham? Is there any connection (besides the one by train) between Canons Park and Cannon Street?

Since the first edition of this book was published in 1977, a few entries have had the benefit of new information. Furthermore, it should be borne in mind that some derivations are subject to dispute and, where appropriate, I have given two or three alternative explanations.

Station opening dates shown at the end of each entry record the introduction of passenger services by London Underground or its predecessors. A new feature of this edition is the inclusion of alternative names planned or considered before openings. Stations on the Docklands Light Railway are covered in a separate chapter.

Cyril M. Harris
April 2001

Acknowledgements

The author would like to thank: the publicity staff of the former London Transport Executive for their help. The County Archivist of Essex County Council, London's many librarians for their assistance, Charles E. Lee for checking the numerous transport dates, Alan Pearce for checking the Docklands Light Rail entries, my late mother, Mrs Hilda Harris, for her many hours of reading and checking proofs. And, finally, a number of London citizens for their help and assistance.

A

Acton Town was recorded as *Acton*(e) in 1181 and the name is derived from the Old English *ac*, 'oak' and *tun*, 'a farm' – meaning 'the farm by the oak tree(s)'. There was a busy little village in this area from the 16th century onwards developing into the *town* of *Acton*. It has been known as Church Acton to distinguish it from East Acton, formerly a separate hamlet.

The station was built as MILL HILL PARK on 1 July 1879; rebuilt with the name MILL HILL PARK on 20 February 1910; but re-named ACTON TOWN on 1 March 1910.

Aldgate is named after the gate which once spanned the road between Dukes Place and Jewry Street. The original gate was built by the Saxons and the name is derived from *Aelgate* – meaning 'open to all' a free gate. It has also been interpreted as the *old-gate* but this is probably incorrect. *Aldgate* was one of the original four gates in the City Wall, rebuilt in 1609 but demolished in 1761.

The station was opened as ALDGATE on 18 November 1876.

Aldgate East – see Aldgate.

The proposed name of the original station was COMMERCIAL ROAD, but it opened as ALDGATE EAST on 6 October 1884. The station was moved a short distance east in 1938.

Alperton originally *Ealhberhington*, was recorded as *Alprinton* in the 12th century and the name is derived from the personal name of the Saxon *Ealhbeart* and Old English *tun*, 'a farm' – means 'the farm of Ealhbeart' and his family who once lived on a site here. It is sometimes recorded that *Alperton* is derived from 'apple farm', but this can be discounted. The name changed to Alperton in the course of time.

The station was opened as PERIVALE-ALPERTON on 28 June 1903 and re-named ALPERTON on 7 October 1910.

Amersham was recorded as *Agmondesham* in 1066 and the name is derived from the original wording *Ealgmundsham*, being the personal name of the Saxon *Ealgmund*, and Old English *ham*, a homestead – 'the home of Ealgmund' and his family who once lived on a site here. Changed to Amersham c. 1675.

The station was opened as AMERSHAM on 1 September 1892. it was re-named AMERSHAM & CHESHAM BOIS on 12 March 1922, reverting to AMERSHAM in about 1934.

Angel. This district and road junction at the end of City Road takes its name from a once famous coaching inn that dates from at least 1638.

The *Angel* was one of the commonest mediæval inn signs and in the mid-18th century there were 23 Angel Alleys and 30 Angel Courts in London. The building now stands empty and little noticed on the corner of Pentonville Road and Islington High Street. The only indication of its past history is *Angel Mews*, which runs behind the building.

The station was opened as Angel on 17 November 1901 and was completely rebuilt in 1992 to cope with a much higher usage.

Archway. In 1813 the Archway Road was constructed to avoid the slope up to Highgate Hill. The viaduct was designed by Sir Alexander Binnie and built in 1897 over the road in place of the former *Highgate Archway* which was a short tunnel. The district is, therefore, known as Archway. Railings, seven feet high, were erected on the viaduct to discourage the many suicides that took place here, but the view is still spectacular.

The station was opened as Highgate on 22 June 1907, although Archway Tavern appears on at least one pre-opening map. With the building of the northern extension to form an interchange with Highgate LNER, Highgate South was considered before the name was changed to Archway (Highgate) on 11 June 1939, and Archway in December 1947.

Arnos Grove was recorded as *Arnold(e)s* Grove in 1551 and it seems that the name should be associated with the 14th-century family of Margery *Arnold* who once lived in this area. The *Grove* itself runs to the north of the nearby Arnos Park.

The station's name was planned to be Bowes Road, but it opened as Arnos Grove on 19 September 1932.

Arsenal takes its name from the famous *Arsenal Football Club* which moved here in 1913 from Woolwich where it had been founded at the Royal Arsenal Factory in 1884 – hence the nickname for the team: The Gunners.

The station was opened as Gillespie Road on 15 December 1906 and re-named Arsenal on 31 October 1932 at a pre-war height of the Club's fame.

B

Baker Street was completed in 1799 and was named after either Sir Edward *Baker* of Ranston in Dorset who was the owner of an estate in the area, or more probably, William *Baker* who developed an estate after purchasing land from William Portman (who owned the whole area) in the eighteenth century. The street is, of course, associated with the famous fictional detective Sherlock Holmes 'who had rooms at 221b Baker Street'.

The Metropolitan Line station was opened as BAKER STREET on 10 January 1863, the 'extension' line station opened on 13 April 1868, and the Bakerloo Line station on 10 March 1906.

Balham was known as *Baelenham* in 957 and later as *Bealganhamm* being derived from the personal name of the Saxon *Bealga*, and Old English *ham*, 'a homestead'. It means 'the home of Bealga' and his family who once lived on a site here. It was recorded as *Balgaham* in c.1115.

The station was opened as BALHAM on 6 December 1926.

Bank takes its name from the *Bank of England* which was established in 1694 based on the proposals of William Paterson, a Scotsman. From 1694-1724 the business of the Bank was carried on at Mercers' Hall, and then at Grocers' Hall. In 1724 a site in Threadneedle Street was purchased; the building was erected in 1732-4 and rebuilt in 1940.

Baker Street station about 1906.

Baker St Station.

Balham High Street, showing the railway bridge carrying the LBSC main line between Victoria and Brighton. The Northern Line station would be erected beside the bridge about twenty years after this photograph was taken.

Threadneedle Street was recorded in 1598 as *Three needle Street*; this probably refers to a tailor's sign, for this area was once an enclave of tailors and drapers, or a children's game '*threadneedle*', first noticed in 1751 but which may be two centuries older. There is no evidence that the street was ever the centre for the Needlemakers' Company.

The Waterloo & City Railway was opened by the Duke of Cambridge on 11 July 1898 which was the 50th anniversary of the opening of the original Waterloo Station. The City Station was called CITY, although sometimes referred to as MANSION HOUSE. It was not re-named BANK until 28 October 1940. The Northern Line station was opened as BANK on 25 February 1900, LOMBARD STREET having been its planned name at one stage, followed by the Central Line BANK station on 30 July 1900. The re-constructed station was opened on 5 May 1925.

Barbican was called *barbicana* when a Roman Tower once stood just north of the street that now bears this name. *Barbicana* is Latin in origin and, in its turn, is probably from the Persian wording meaning 'upper chamber'. The Saxons named the tower *burgh kennin* – meaning 'town watchtower', on which for many centuries fires were lit to guide travellers to their destinations across London. It seems the tower was pulled down in 1267 on the orders of Henry III but it was then rebuilt in 1336 on the orders of Edward III. The date when the tower was finally demolished is uncertain but it is known there was a house on the site in 1720. The area has been extensively re-developed since the Second World War as the *Barbican Project*.

The station was opened as ALDERSGATE STREET on 23 December 1865; re-named ALDERSGATE & BARBICAN 1923, and BARBICAN on 1 December 1968.

Barking was recorded as *Berecingum* in 735 and is probabl named from the Saxon people the *Bercia* and the Old English place name word ending *ing*, literally 'the people who lived at'. Barking, we can deduce, means – 'the home of the Bercias'. The area was divided into various manors during the Middle Ages, one being Berengers, a variation on the original name. It is also possible that the name can be interpreted as 'the dwellers among the birch trees' and, maybe, this referred to the Bercias.

The station was opened as BARKING by the London, Tilbury & Southend Railway on 13 April 1854 and first used by Underground trains on 2 June 1902.

Barkingside was so named in 1538 being on the extreme edge of the old parish of Barking. The word *side* is associated with a slope or hill especially one extending for a considerable distance, which was no doubt the case during the 16th century.

The station was opened as BARKINGSIDE by the Great Eastern Railway on 1 May 1903 and first used by Underground trains on 31 May 1948.

Barons Court. Unlike Earl's Court this name has no connection with the law, or the nobility, but was so named after an estate that extends from the District Line to Perham Road to the south. The estate was planned by Sir William Palliser and built at the end of the 19th century. The name was fabricated-perhaps in allusion to the title of *Court Baron* then held by the Lord of the Manor or because Earl's Court was the name of a nearby district.

The station was opened as BARONS COURT on 9 October 1905.

Bayswater was recorded as *Bayard's Watering* in 1380 and has had many variant spellings before being named as *Bay(e)swater* by 1659. The original *Bayard's Watering* was the place where the Westbourne Stream crossed the Oxford Road (now Bayswater Road) and is possibly derived from the *Bayard* family who once lived in this area.

The station was opened as BAYSWATER on 1 October 1868. Later known as BAYSWATER (QUEEN'S ROAD) and then QUEEN'S ROAD, BAYSWATER. Re-named BAYSWATER (QUEEN'S ROAD) & WESTBOURNE GROVE on 20 July 1922. The name reverted to BAYSWATER in 1933.

Becontree is thought to take its name from a local natural feature although associated with the Saxon people the *Beohha* who had an encampment by a distinctive tree, which was probably a boundary mark. It was recorded as *Beuentreu* in Domesday Book. It is possible, however, that the name is from Old English, *beacen-treo(w)*, 'beacon tree' being an old meeting place.

The station was opened as GALE STREET by the London Midland & Scottish Railway on 28 June 1926; re-named BECONTREE 18 July 1932. Used by Underground trains from 12 September 1932.

Belsize Park is one of a number of similarly styled tube stations dating from 1906/07.

Belsize Park was recorded as *Balassis* in 1317 from the Old French wording *bel asis*, which means 'beautifully situated', and was no doubt aptly named from the manor house and park which were once on the present site of Belsize Square. No fewer than ten streets in this part of north west London include *Belsize* in their name.

Before the station opened plain BELSIZE was considered for the name, but it was opened as BELSIZE PARK on 22 June 1907.

Bermondsey was recorded as *Vermudesi* c.712 and as *Bermundesy* in the Domesday Book and the name is derived from the Saxon lord of the district, *Beormund* and his family who lived here and the Old English *Eg* – 'an island' (or marsh) – 'Beormunds island'. The name changed to its present spelling over time.

The station opened as BERMONDSEY on 17 September 1999.

Bethnal Green. *Blithehale* was the recorded name for this district during the 13th century. The second element *hale* means – 'an angle or corner of land'. Maybe *Blithe* is a corruption of the personal name *Blida*, a family who resided here in the reign of Edward I (1272–1307), or perhaps refers to an ancient stream of this area called *Bythe*. The 'village green at Bathon's river meadow' could be the complete meaning of the name. It has had many changes of spelling until recorded as *Bethnal Greene* in 1657. On what remains of the *Green* now stand St John's Church (built in 1825–8), the Bethnal Green Museum and the local public gardens.

The committee of the New Works Programme 1935/40 considered the name of Bethnal to avoid confusion with the LNER station of Bethnal Green Junction, although when the station opened as Bethnal Green on 4 December 1946 the LNER had adopted the same name for their own station.

Blackfriars. This area takes its name from the colour of the habits worn by the friars of a Dominican monastery who were known as the *Black Friars*. The monastery was established during the 13th century by the Earl of Kent, but was closed on the orders of Henry VIII in 1538. Part of the building later became the *Blackfriars Theatre* which was pulled down in 1665.

The station is built on the site of Chatham Place which was named in honour of William Pitt, 1st Earl of Chatham.

The station was opened as Blackfriars on 30 May 1870.

Blackfriars Bridge with the dome of St Paul's Cathedral in the background and Blackfriars South Eastern Railway station to the left of it. The District Railway's station neighbours it.

The original entrance to the Central London Railway's Bond Street station situated in Oxford Street. At the time of this photograph, the Underground house style has made a small appearance, on posters and on the lampshades between the arches.

Blackhorse Road was recorded as *Black House Lane* in 1848 which is the correct spelling, for the road takes its name from an old *Black House*, being on the site of an old Clock House. Changed to *Blackhorse Lane* (then road) at a later date, this change has some connection with the east London dialect.

The station was opened as BLACKHORSE ROAD on 1 September 1968.

Bond Street was laid out in 1686 to designs by Sir Thomas *Bond*, Comptroller of the Household of Queen Henrietta Maria (The Queen Mother), and is named after him, although he died in 1685. The street is now renowned for its fashionable shops and picture dealers' galleries. The south portion of the street is known as *Old Bond Street*, being re-named in 1734, while the north portion running to Oxford Street is known as *New Bond Street*, named in 1732.

Before the station opened, the name DAVIES STREET was proposed, but it opened as BOND STREET on 24 September 1900.

Borough. This district is part of ancient London, for here the Romans founded a settlement and built a 'high street' as an approach road to London Bridge. The *Borough* is a small part of Southwark and although the word borough means 'a fortified place' (Old English *burh*) the word now has another definition. It also refers to a town with its own local government, for in the late Middle Ages this was the only London Borough both outside the City Wall and sending its own Member to Parliament. It has kept its name ever since.

The station was opened as BOROUGH on 18 December 1890.

Boston Manor. This *Boston* has no connection with its more famous namesakes in Lincolnshire or the USA. Known during the 14th century as *Bordeston* from *Bords* (a personal name) and Old English *tun*, 'a farm – means 'Bords farm', which in its turn has been corrupted to *Burston*, then *Boston* during the 16th century. The *Manor* originally belonged to the convent of St Helen's Bishopsgate and its ownership has changed hands many times during the course of history. *Boston Manor* is noted for its Tudor and Jacobean Mansion – 'Boston House'.

The station was opened on 1 May 1883 as BOSTON ROAD, re-named BOSTON MANOR on 11 December 1911, and the rebuilt station was completed 25 March 1934.

Bounds Green is a district of North London whose name is derived from its association with the families of John le *Bonde* in 1294 and Walter le *Bounde* during the 13th century and being recorded as *le Boundes* in 1365. *Bounds Green* is the modern version of the name. Nothing is left of the *Green*, the area now occupied by the Bounds Green Road.

Prior to the opening of the station the name of BROWNLOW ROAD was proposed, but it opened as BOUNDS GREEN on 19 September 1932.

Bow Road. This main road is so called from an arched ('bow') bridge built over the River Lea in the 12th century; or from the *bow* (or bend) in the road to the east of the station, which can still be seen just to the west of the modern fly-over.

The station was opened as BOW ROAD on 11 June 1902.

Brent Cross takes its name from the nearby river that joins the Thames at Brentford and was recorded as *Braegente* in 959. In its turn the river-name is derived from the hypothetical Old English *Brigantica*, probably meaning the holy or high river and as the river flows mostly through low country the former is most likely. The name became *Brent*(e) by the 13th century.

The station was originally proposed to have been named WOODSTOCK, but it was opened as BRENT on 19 November 1923 and re-named BRENT CROSS on 20 July 1976.

Brixton is recorded as *brixges stane* in 1062, and as *Brixistan* in the Domesday Book. The name is derived from the personal name of the Saxon *Beorhtric* and the Old English *stane*, 'stone'. Stones were often used as meeting points. The name changed to Brixton in the course of time.

The station was opened as BRIXTON on 23 July 1971.

Bromley-by-Bow. Bromley was recorded as *Braembelege* in 1000, *Brambeley* in 1128 and is derived from the Old English *broom* (tree) and *leah*, 'a forest'. See Bow Road for origin of the second part of the name.

The station was opened by the London, Tilbury & Southend Railway on 31 March 1858 as BROMLEY. It was first used by Underground trains on 2 June 1902 and was re-named BROMLEY-BY-BOW on 5 May 1968.

Buckhurst Hill, as the name suggests, takes its name from a local natural feature, recorded as *Bocherst(e)* in 1135 from the Old English *beech* (tree) and *hyrst*, 'a copse' or 'wood' – later to be called *Buckhurst*. The area has also been called *Goldhurst*, the 'gold' referring no doubt to the colour of the trees in the wood. The *Hill* refers to another nearby feature.

The station was opened as BUCKHURST HILL by the Eastern Counties Railway on 22 August 1856 and first used by Underground trains on 21 November 1948.

Burnt Oak. Tradition has it that the Romans had a site near here which they used as a boundary mark where fires were lit as a guide – so a *burnt oak*.

Prior to the opening of the station the name SHEAVES HILL was proposed. This was not liked by Hendon Urban District Council, who suggested BURNT OAK, ORANGE HILL or DEANSBROOK. The station opened as BURNT OAK on 27 October 1924.

Brixton before the First World War. The site of the present day Underground station is on the right, but Brixton would have to wait another half century for the Victoria Line to arrive.

C

Caledonian Road was constructed c.1826 and is named from the *Caledonian Asylum* for Scottish children established on a site nearby in 1815. The road was referred to as the 'New Road from Battle Bridge to Holloway' in 1841.

Prior to the station's opening, the name of BARNSBURY was considered, but it opened as CALEDONIAN ROAD on 15 December 1906.

Camden Town. This area of north west London was built c.1791, and was once a manor belonging to St Paul's Cathedral. The manor was obtained, by marriage, in 1795 by Charles Pratt, Earl of *Camden*, of Camden Place in Kent, and is so named. The Earl allowed his land to be leased for building houses, so in the course of time *Camden Town* came into use.

Prior to the station's opening, the name of CAMDEN ROAD was considered, but it opened as CAMDEN TOWN on 22 June 1907.

Canada Water is a new development in this area and it takes its name from the original Canada Docks which were built in 1876.

The station opened as CANADA WATER on 17 September 1999.

Canary Wharf was built in 1936 and the then owners of the wharf, *Fruit Lines Limited*, built a warehouse for their imports of fruits from the Canary Islands and the Mediterranean in 1937, hence the name.

The station opened as CANARY WHARF on 17 September 1999.

Canary Wharf before the massive docklands development.

Barking Road at Canning Town in the 1920s.

Canning Town is the industrial and residential district built up during the 1850s to house the labourers working in the nearby Victoria Docks. It has been suggested that the town is named in honour of Lord Canning (a former Governor General of India) but this can be discounted. In fact the town takes it name from an industrial firm which was once centred in this area.

The original Great Eastern Railway station was opened on the south side of the Barking Road as CANNING TOWN in 1847, being moved to its present site in 1888. The adjacent Jubilee Line station was opened as CANNING TOWN on 14 May 1999.

Cannon Street has no connection with guns or even billiards as the name might suggest, for the candle-makers and wick-chandlers who made their wares for the Church lived here in the late Middle Ages. It was first mentioned in the records of c.1180 as *Candelwichstrete* (from *Candle* and Old English *wic*, 'a dwelling'). Through a series of name-shortenings and the Cockney dialect the name was contracted to *Cannon Street* by the mid-17th century and this modern form was noted by Pepys in his famous diary in 1667. On the site of the present mainline station was once the Steelyard, a store to which members of the German Hanseatic League once brought their goods for sale.

The main line station was opened by the South Eastern Railway on 1 September 1866. The Underground station was opened also as CANNON STREET on 6 October 1884.

Canons Park. Six acres of this area were granted to the Prior of the St Augustinian canons of St Bartholomew's, Smithfield, in 1331 and were recorded as *Canons* during the 16th century. *Canons Park* later became the property of the Duke of Chandos and on the estate was built the Duke's magnificent mansion (also named 'Canons') which was demolished after its sale by the Duke's heir in 1747, being broken up and sold by lots at auction.

The station was opened on 10 December 1932 as CANONS PARK (EDGWARE), becoming just CANONS PARK during 1933.

Chalfont & Latimer. Chalfont was recorded as *Ceadeles funta* in 949 from the personal name of a Saxon, *Ceadel*, and Old Welsh *funta*, 'a spring or stream' – 'Ceadel's home near a spring'. *Latimer* is also derived from a personal name, recorded as *Yselhamstede* in 1220 and *Isenhampstede Latyer* in 1389, from William *Latymer*, who obtained the manor on this site in 1330; the name was over time shortened to *Latimer*.

The station was opened as CHALFONT ROAD on 8 July 1889 and re-named CHALFONT & LATIMER in November 1915.

Chalk Farm. It has been suggested this is a corruption of the wording *Chalcot Farm* but there is no evidence that a farm ever existed in this area. Recorded as *Chaldecot(e)* in 1253, it is stated that this name is derived from cold cottages, referring to the slopes of nearby Haverstock Hill which were bleak and exposed in the early days of settlement in this area. It seems that there was also a place of shelter here for travellers to London.

Prior to the opening of the station the name ADELAIDE ROAD was suggested, but it opened as CHALK FARM on 22 June 1907.

Chancery Lane was constructed by the Knights Templars c.1160 and has a long history with many changes of name. It was recorded as Newstrate (New Street) in the early part of the 13th century. During the reign of Henry III (1216–72) a house was erected on the eastern side of the lane for the conversion of Jews to the Christian faith. The house became famous and Newstrate became *Convers Lane*. Towards the end of the 13th century, Edward I banished the Jews from the country and the house was used by 'the Keeper of the Rolls', where the official records of the Inns of Chancery were kept and once again the name of the street was changed to *Chancellor's Lane* and was recorded as this in 1320. Eventually this name was superseded (once again) by *Chancery Lane*, c.1454 and it seems to imply that the Chancellor (of the Rolls) had a personal office or residence in the Lane.

The station was opened as CHANCERY LANE on 30 July 1900. After extensive re-construction, a new station was opened as CHANCERY LANE (GRAYS INN) on 25 June 1934, gradually reverting to just CHANCERY LANE.

Charing Cross. By tradition, it is said that Edward I in 1291 set up a stone cross near what is now the courtyard of the main-line station to mark the last resting place of the funeral cortege of his Queen Eleanor as it passed from Harby to Westminster – hence the *Cross* part of the name which was recorded as the *stone cross* of *Cherryngge* during the 14th century. There was a little village here named *Cyrringe* c.1000 and the name is derived from the Old English *cierring*, 'turning' or 'to turn', probably referring to the bend in the river Thames nearby. *Charing Cross Road* was built in the 1880s.

Charing Cross early in the twentieth century, looking east down the Strand.

The Bakerloo Line station was opened as TRAFALGAR SQUARE on 10 March 1906. The Northern Line station was opened as CHARING CROSS on 22 June 1907, being re-named CHARING CROSS (STRAND) on 6 April 1914 and further re-named STRAND on 9 May 1915 until being closed for re-building on 4 June 1973. The combined station serving the Bakerloo, Northern and Jubilee lines was named CHARING CROSS from 1 May 1979.

Chesham had an early association with the Old English word *ceaster* – signifying 'a Roman town and fortification'. Recorded during the 10th century as *Caesteshamm* from the Old English *ceastel*, literally 'a heap of stones', and *hamm*, a water meadow' – meaning 'a boundary mark by a spring'. In the course of time the name has changed to *Chesham*, and nearby is the river Chess.

The station was opened as Chesham on 8 July 1889.

Chigwell was recorded as *Cingheuuella* in the Domesday Book and may be is associated with a Saxon named *Cicea*. But the name is probably derived from Old English *ceaege*, 'gorse' and *weg*, 'well' – 'the well within the shingle'. The name has changed in the course of time to *Chigwell*.

The station was opened as Chigwell by the Great Eastern Railway on 1 May 1903 and first used by Underground trains on 21 November 1948.

Chiswick Park. Recorded as *Ceswican* c.1000. Chiswick has had various spellings throughout time, and is thought to derive from the Old English *cese*, 'cheese' and *wic*, 'farm'. Although there are parks nearby the station, they are not connected with the original park.

The station was opened as Acton Green on 1 July 1879; re-named Chiswick Park & Acton Green in March 1887; and Chiswick Park on 1 March 1910.

Chorleywood. The Old English word for a free peasant lower than the rank of nobleman was *ceorl* and these people once had an encampment on a site near here. Recorded as *Charlewoode* in 1524 although the name is of an earlier origin and is derived from the Old English *ceorl* (the group name of the people) and *leah*, a wood' – 'the wood or clearing of the free peasants' and known as *Chorley Wood* by 1730.

The station opened as Chorley Wood on 8 July 1889, and was re-named Chorley Wood & Chenies in November 1915. It reverted to Chorley Wood during 1934 until about 1964 when the single word Chorleywood appeared on maps and later on platform signs.

Clapham Common. There was an ancient village on the site of the present *Clapham*, recorded as *Cloppaham* c.880 and as *Clopeham* in the Domesday Book. The name is derived from the Old English *clap*, 'a hill' and *ham*, 'home' – this wording for hill usually refers to one on stubby ground. The *Common* was called *Clapham Common* in 1718 and the meaning of the word is a track of open land used in *common* by the inhabitants of the town.

The station was opened as CLAPHAM COMMON on 3 June 1900.

Clapham North – see Clapham Common.

The station was opened as CLAPHAM ROAD on 3 June 1900 and re-named CLAPHAM NORTH 13 September 1926.

Clapham South – see Clapham Common.

The name of NIGHTINGALE LANE was chosen first, but the station opened as CLAPHAM SOUTH on 13 September 1926.

Cockfosters. This district of north London was recorded as *Cockfosters* in 1524 and although the origin of the name is uncertain, it is possible that it is derived from either the personal name of a family that once lived here, or a house recorded in

The site of Cockfosters station c.1931.

1613 on the edge of Enfield Chase and called **Cockfosters**. It is suggested that this was the residence of the chief *forester* (or cock forester), hence this rather unusual name which, until the arrival of the tube, was sometimes spelt as two words.

Prior to the station's opening the name of TRENT PARK was considered, but it opened as COCKFOSTERS on 31 July 1933.

Colindale was recorded as *Collyndene* in 1550, *Collins Deepe* in 1710 and probably should be associated with the family of a John *Collin* who once lived here. The 'Deep' must refer to the valley of the nearby Silk Stream (later changed to *Dale*, from the Old English *dael*, 'a valley'). *Colindale*, therefore, means 'the home of the Collins Family in the valley'.

The station was opened as COLINDALE on 18 August 1924.

Colliers Wood takes its name from the *Colliers* or 'charcoal burners' who worked in this area during the 16th century.

The station opened as Colliers Wood on 13 September 1926.

Covent Garden was originally the walled enclosure and garden belonging to the monks of Westminster Abbey, recorded in 1491 as *Convent Garden* (from Old French *couvent*), which stretched from Long Acre to the Strand. After the dissolution of the monasteries the site was claimed by the Crown and sold to the 1st Earl of Bedford in 1552 who had a house built here, while the 4th Earl had the area laid out as a residential quarter. *Covent Garden* was famous for its fruit market established in 1661, now moved to a site at Vauxhall in south London, and for its Royal Opera House, the third and present one on this site being built in 1858.

The station was opened as Covent Garden on 11 April 1907.

Croxley. The name is derived from the Old English *crocs*, 'a clearing' and *leah*, 'a forest' – means 'the clearing in the forest'. It was recorded as *Crokesleya* in 1166 with variant spellings until 1750 when it was known as *Crosley* (*Green*).

The station was opened as Croxley Green on 2 November 1925 and re-named Croxley on 23 May 1949.

The bustle that was Covent Garden when it was a fruit and vegetable market. This was the scene in the 1940s. The flower market – now London's Transport Museum – is in the background.

D

Dagenham East. The name *Dagenham* was originally recorded as *Daccanhamm* in 692 and is derived from the personal name of the Saxon *Daecca* and the Old English *ham*, 'a homestead' and means 'the home of Decca' and his family, that once lived on a site here. It was recorded as *Dakenham* in 1254.

The station was opened as DAGENHAM by the London, Tilbury & Southend Railway on 1 May 1885, and was first used by Underground trains on 2 June 1902. It was re-named DAGENHAM EAST on 1 May 1949.

The shopping centre at Dagenham as it appeared in the early 1930s.

Dagenham Heathway – see Dagenham East. The *Heathway* as the name suggests takes its name from the road that runs to the north, through Dagenham to Becontree Heath.

The station was opened as HEATHWAY on 12 September 1932 and re-named DAGENHAM HEATHWAY in May 1949.

Debden takes its name from a natural location of the area and is recorded as *Deppendana* in the Domesday Book. It is derived from the Old English *deb*, 'deep' and *den*, 'valley' – which means simply 'the deep valley'. It was recorded as *Depeden* in 1227.

The station was opened by the Great Eastern Railway as CHIGWELL ROAD on 24 April 1865, and re-named CHIGWELL LANE on 1 December 1865. It was again re-named as DEBDEN on 25 September 1949 when first used by Underground trains.

Dollis Hill was recorded as *Daleson Hill* in 1593 and later as *Dolly's Hill*, but the name origin is unknown; possibly it is taken from a nearby manor that was once here. Dollis Hill Lane, the main road, climbs the *Hill* at this point.

The station was opened as DOLLIS HILL on 1 October 1909.

E

The Mall, Ealing.

Close to Ealing Broadway station is The Mall, forming part of the Uxbridge Road, along which the trams ran between Shepherd's Bush and Uxbridge until replaced by trolleybuses in 1936. When this scene was photographed the redundant tram tracks had been covered by strips of tar prior to their removal.

Ealing Broadway. *Gillingas* was recorded for this area c.698 and is derived from the Saxon people the *Gilla* and the Old English place name word ending, *ing*, literally, 'the people who lived at'. It has had many changes of spelling – *Ilingis* c.1127, then *Yealing* to *Ealing* in 1622. The *Broadway* is the main road beside the station.

The District Line station, adjoining that of the GWR, opened as Ealing Broadway on 1 July 1879, Central Line platforms being added on 3 August 1920.

Ealing Common – see Ealing Broadway. The *Common* lies to the south of the station – see under Clapham Common for meaning of 'common'.

The station was opened on 1 July 1879 as Ealing Common; re-named Ealing Common & West Acton in 1886; and reverted to Ealing Common on 1 March 1910.

Earl's Court. After the Conquest the De Vere family were granted the Manor of Kensington which at one time had a *court* house. Later the head of the family was created Earl of Oxford, hence the name *Earl's Court*. The old Court stood beside a little lane which is still called Old Manor Yard, but the court building was demolished in 1886. Now on the site are Barkston and Bramham Gardens.

The station was opened as EARL'S COURT on 31 October 1871, burnt down 30 December 1875 and repaired temporarily; new station further west opened 1 February 1878.

East Acton – see Acton Town for meaning of name. *East Acton* was formerly a separate hamlet from Acton and was recorded as *Estacton* in 1294.

The station was opened as EAST ACTON on 3 August 1920.

Eastcote was known as *Estcotte* during the 13th century and the name is only slightly changed in the course of time. The name is derived from the Old English *cote*, 'cottage' or 'shelter' and means 'the cottage(s) to the east', literally the hamlet to the east of Ruislip, for there was once a Westcott also.

The station was opened as EASTCOTE on 26 May 1906.

East Finchley – see Finchley Central.

The station was opened as EAST FINCHLEY on 22 August 1867 and was first used by Underground trains on 3 July 1939.

East Ham was recorded as *Hamme* in 958 which signifies that this and West Ham comprised one single geographical location and not until 1206 was the name *Eastham* recorded. The name is derived from the Old English *hamm*, 'a water meadow' – refer-ring to the low-lying riverside meadow near the bend of the Thames. (See also West Ham.)

The station was opened as EAST HAM by the London, Tilbury & Southend Railway on 31 March 1858; first used by Underground trains on 2 June 1902.

East Ham soon after laying of tramlines along its High Street in 1901.

East Putney – see Putney Bridge.

The station was opened as EAST PUTNEY by the London & South Western Railway on 3 June 1889 and was served by District Line trains from that date.

Edgware was recorded *Aegces Wer* in 972–8 and *Eggeswera* later and is derived from the personal name of a Saxon *Ecgis* and weir – means very simply, 'Ecgis', fishing pool from a local stretch of water. From an early set of boundaries the precise position of the fishing pool can be ascertained; it is where Watling Street (now Edgware Road) crosses the Edgware Brook.

The station was opened as EDGWARE on 18 August 1924.

Edgware Road was once part of the Roman road called *Watling Street* that ran from Dover through London to St Albans. During the 18th century the road became *Edgware Road*, being the direct route from Marble Arch to Edgware, which lies to the north west. Until the early 1900s it was often spelt *Edgeware*.

The Metropolitan Line station was opened as EDGWARE ROAD on 10 January 1863; the separate Bakerloo Line station was opened as EDGWARE ROAD on 15 June 1907.

Elephant & Castle is named after an old tavern which was originally on the site of a 16th-century playhouse, the 'Newington Theatre', which staged many of Shakespeare's plays. Later converted into a tavern and, during the 18th century, to a posting house and inn, being rebuilt in 1816 and again in 1898. The tavern had a gilt model of an *elephant and castle* on its frontage, which was preserved when the building was demolished in 1959, and is now displayed in the nearby shopping centre. The sign originated from the badge of the Cutler's Company who adopted the elephant as its device in 1445 when at the marriage of Henry VI to Queen Margaret the members of the Company wore elephants as decorations upon their coats or shields; this may have represented the ivory used by cutlers for their craft. The theory that the name is a corruption of *The Infanta of Castile* has no historical foundation. The present day 'pub' stands a short distance from the old site.

The Northern Line station opened as ELEPHANT & CASTLE on 18 December 1890; the Bakerloo Line station on 5 August 1906.

Elm Park, as the name suggests, takes its name from natural local woodland and was perhaps a meeting place of the local inhabitants long ago.

The station was opened as ELM PARK on 13 May 1935.

The Victoria Embankment, connecting Westminster and Blackfriars bridges, was built in conjunction with the construction of the Metropolitan District Railway, opened in 1868. This view is from Hungerford Bridge.

Embankment. The Embankment is the roadway by the River Thames. In 1863 an Act of Parliament was passed for the building of the embankments and work started immediately on the new Victoria Embankment between Westminster and the Temple. It was completed and opened to the public in 1870.

The District Line station was opened as CHARING CROSS on 30 May 1870. The Bakerloo Line station, opened on 10 March 1906, was first named EMBANKMENT; then re-named CHARING CROSS (EMBANKMENT) on 6 April 1914 when the Northern Line platforms were opened. The combined station was named CHARING CROSS on 9 May 1915. It was re-named CHARING CROSS EMBANKMENT on 4 August 1974, being further re-named as EMBANKMENT on 12 September 1976.

Epping was recorded as *Eppinges* in the Domesday Book from the people known as the *Yippinga*, derived from the Old English *yppe*, 'a raised place' and the *ing* word ending (literally 'the people who lived here') and means 'The people who live on the uplands', referring also to a look-out post they had here. It was recorded as *Upping* in 1227, then *Epping*.

The station was opened as EPPING by the Great Eastern Railway on 24 April 1865 and first used by Underground trains on 25 September 1949. Since 30 September 1994 Epping has been the eastern terminus of the Central Line, the Ongar branch having closed on that date.

The original platforms at Euston City & South London station, showing
locomotive hauled rolling stock. The island platform with tracks either side
lasted until the 1960s, when the construction of the Victoria Line necessitated
extensive rebuilding, including this tunnel which retains one track only and an
unusually wide platform.

Euston takes its name from the main-line station, opened on
20 July 1837, which was adjacent to Euston Grove and Euston
Square on the estate held by the Duke of Grafton, whose seat
was at *Euston Hall*, Suffolk.

Prior to the Underground station's opening the name of
MELTON STREET was considered, but the station was opened as
EUSTON on 12 May 1907.

Euston Square was laid out in 1805 and, like *Euston*, takes its
name from the seat of the Duke of Grafton. The station is on the
site of a farm which existed as late as 1830.

The station opened as GOWER STREET on 10 January 1863 and
was re-named EUSTON SQUARE on 1 November 1909.

"The new entrance to the Euston Square railway station" in 1870

Euston main line
station was still
called Euston
Square in this
impression of
1870. The famous
Doric arch is in
the background,
with the newly
built lodges
either side.

F

Fairlop. A legend surrounds the name of Fairlop. In the early part of the 19th century there was a fine oak tree here, which sheltered a long-established fair founded by a certain Daniel Day. When Day died in 1767 his friends, after much consideration, decided to make his coffin from the tree and as the tree continued to flourish, they agreed that they had made a *fair lop*. A little fanciful perhaps, but the name is derived from *fair* and the Modern English *lop* 'a small branch or twig' – and means 'the beautiful trees with their leafy branches' which stood nearby.

The station was opened as FAIRLOP by the Great Eastern Railway on 1 May 1903 and first used by Underground trains on 31 May 1948.

Farringdon. This part of central London takes its name from *Farringdon Street*. In 1279 the City merchant William de Farindon of the Goldsmiths' Company purchased the 'ward' of this area and became an Alderman of it two years later; the street was named in his honour. The street was built in 1738 upon arches, above the old River Fleet which is now a sewer.

The station was opened on 10 January 1863 as FARRINGDON STREET; re-named FARRINGDON & HIGH HOLBORN 26 January 1922; became FARRINGDON on 21 April 1936.

Farringdon & High Holborn is proclaimed along the top of the building in the style used by the Metropolitan Railway on many of its stations. This picture was taken after London Transport had reduced the name to Farringdon, there no longer being the need to make the claim of serving High Holborn when the Central Line stations were closer.

Finchley Central was recorded as *Finchelee-leya* c.1208 and it is possible that the name is derived from what can be interpreted as a *finch clearing* (meaning the bird) and the Old English *leah*, 'a forest' – 'the clearing in the forest with the finches'. More likely, the wording is from a personal name, *Finc* – meaning 'Finc's Forest'. The name has many spellings and was recorded as *Fyncheley* in 1547.

The station was opened by the Great Northern Railway as Finchley & Hendon on 22 August 1867; it became Finchley (Church End) on 1 February 1894 and Finchley Central on 1 April 1940; it was first used by Underground trains on 14 April 1940.

Finchley Road. In 1827 an Act of Parliament was passed to build a new road out of London to Barnet, to avoid the hills of Hampstead and Highgate. This road was planned by way of *Finchley* – hence the name.

The station was opened as Finchley Road on 30 June 1879.

Finsbury Park is on the site of the earlier *Hornsey Wood*. The Park, opened in 1869, was so called because the inhabitants within the old Parliamentary borough of Finsbury initiated a movement for its acquisition, which all seems very curious since it is far from Finsbury, which is near central London. *Finsbury* itself was recorded as *Vinisbir* in 1231 and this is most likely to have been derived from an Anglo-Scandinavian name *Fin*, and the Old English *burgh*, 'manor' – and thus means 'Fin's Manor'. It was recorded as *Fenysbury* in 1535.

The station was opened by the Great Northern Railway as Seven Sisters Road on 1 July 1861. It was renamed Finsbury Park in 1869 and first served by the Piccadilly Line on 15 December 1906.

Fulham Broadway. The manor of *Fulanham* is recorded as early as 691. There has been much speculation about the origin of the name, two explanations being *foul-town* on account of its muddy ways near the river, or *fowl-ham* – being the haunt of wild-fowl. Both of these explanations can now be discounted. It is more likely that *Fulham* is derived from the personal name *Fulla* and the Old English *hamm*, 'a water meadow', being descriptive of the low-lying bend in the River Thames at this point – 'The Meadow where Fulla lives', referring to an early Saxon and his family. It has had many changes in spelling and was recorded as *Fullam* in 1533.

The station was opened as Walham Green on 1 March 1880; re-named Fulham Broadway 2 March 1952.

G

Gants Hill was recorded as *Gantesgave* in 1291 and the name may well be associated with the family of Richard le *Gant*.

At the planning stage of the New Works Programme 1935/40, the station was referred to as ILFORD NORTH. CRANBROOK was suggested as an alternative, as was GANTS HILL which was not liked by the New Works Committee. However, the station opened as GANTS HILL on 14 December 1947.

Gloucester Road was known as 'Hog moore lane' as late as 1858 and at this time was probably descriptive of a muddy tract. Was re-named in the early 19th century after Maria, Duchess of *Gloucester*, who lived in the road at the turn of the century.

The station was opened as BROMPTON (GLOUCESTER ROAD) on 1 October 1868; re-named GLOUCESTER ROAD 1907.

Golders Green was recorded in 1612 and *Golder* seems clearly to refer to a personal name although no such recorded name has been noted in the early history of the parish. It seems that the name should be associated with John le *Godere* in 1321 and John *Godyer* of Hendon in 1371 and it may well be that Golders is a corruption of the later name. It is also suggested that *Godyer* was an obscure farmer who in fact sold his property and left the district. The *Green* was once part of the fields of Middlesex, which remained rural until the arrival of the railway.

The station was opened as GOLDERS GREEN on 22 June 1907.

When Golders Green station was built, it was surrounded by fields. This entrance in Finchley Road was built after development had occurred.

Goldhawk Road was *Gould Hawk* Lane in 1813 and maybe the road should be associated with a family named *Goldhawk*(e) of the 15th century, for the name is frequently mentioned in 'Court Rolls' of this time. There was also a *Goldhauek* living in nearby Chiswick as early as 1222.

The station was opened as GOLDHAWK ROAD on 1 April 1914.

Goodge Street was once called 'Crab tree field', being a meadow belonging to a widow named Mrs Beresford who married a Marylebone carpenter, John *Goodge* c.1718. When the street was built c.1770 the name was taken from William and Francis *Goodge* who then owned the site.

The station was opened as TOTTENHAM COURT ROAD on 22 June 1907; re-named GOODGE STREET 9 March 1908.

Grange Hill. *The Grange* was one of the manors originally belonging to Tilty Priory. After the dissolution of the monasteries it was granted in 1537 to Thomas Adlington; it changed hands many times until the manor was given as an endowment to Brentwood Grammar School in 1558. The School retained the property until the late 19th century when the land was sold and the building demolished. The *Hill* is the road at the front of the station.

The station was opened as GRANGE HILL by the Great Eastern Railway on 1 May 1903 and was first used by Underground trains on 21 November 1948.

Great Portland Street. In 1710 the manor of Marylebone was bought by the Duke of Newcastle, but by 1734 it passed to the Second Duke of *Portland*. When the street was built in the late 18th century it was so named in honour of the Duke, the northern part being known as *Portland Road*, which was recorded in 1793. The prefix *Great* does not indicate the importance of the street itself but that there are smaller streets of the same name in the neighbourhood.

The station was opened as PORTLAND ROAD on 10 January 1863 and re-named GREAT PORTLAND STREET 1 March 1917.

Greenford was recorded as *grenan forda* in 845 and as *Greneford* in the Domesday Book. As the name suggests, it refers to a *ford*, which was a crossing place over the River Brent which led to a *green*.

The station was opened as GREENFORD by the Great Western Railway on 1 October 1904. A new station for Underground trains was opened on 30 June 1947.

Green Park was created in 1668 and extends north from the Mall and Constitution Hill to Piccadilly; it is 53 acres in size and triangular in shape. Originally added to the Royal Parks by Charles II, it replaced St James's Park as the fashionable resort of society. Reduced in size by George III in 1767 to enlarge the gardens of Buckingham Palace, it was then known occasionally as Upper St James's Park. The name seems to have been derived from the grass that 'grew all around'.

The station was opened as DOVER STREET on 15 December 1906 and re-named GREEN PARK with a re-sited entrance in Piccadilly and next to the park 18 September 1933.

Piccadilly, at the future site of Green Park station entrances on either side of the road, has changed little since the date of this picture in the late 1920s. The station entrance was then in Dover Street.

Gunnersbury. Tradition has it that on a site near here stood the dwelling of *Gunhilda* (or *Gunyld*) the niece of the Danish King Canute (reigned 1016–1035) but this seems to rest on unsupported evidence. Recorded as *Gounyldebury* in 1334 its name seems to be derived, nevertheless, from a female name of Scandinavian origin – *Gunnhild's* (or variations) and the Old English *burh*, 'a manor'. It was recorded as *Gunsbury* in c.1651.

The station was opened by the London & South Western Railway as BRENTFORD ROAD on 1 January 1869 and re-named GUNNERSBURY on 1 November 1871. First used by District and Metropolitan trains on 1 June 1877, the Metropolitan Railway's trains until 31 December 1906.

H

Hainault is not of French origin as it may seem, but is a corruption of the earlier name *Hyneholt*. In its turn this is derived from the Old English *hiwan*, 'a household' and *holt*, 'a wood' (or *hale*, 'a nook of land') – means 'the household on the land with a wood'. The household probably refers to a local religious community. The modern spelling seems to arise from a fictitious connection with a Philippa of *Hainault*.

The station was opened as HAINAULT by the Great Eastern Railway on 1 May 1903. First used by Underground trains (after reconstruction) on 31 May 1948.

Hammersmith was recorded as *Hammersmyth* in 1294 and was a hamlet within Fulham until 1834. The origin of the name is in doubt. Some suggest that it is derived from Old English *ham*, 'a home' or 'town' and *hythe* 'a port' – 'the home by the port', referring to its location on the Thames. More likely it comes from (again Old English) *hamor*, 'hammer' and *smydde* 'a smithy' – referring to a local blacksmith who once lived here. It was recorded as *Hammersmith* in 1675.

The Hammersmith & City Line station was opened as HAMMERSMITH on 13 June 1864, and re-sited farther south on 1 December 1868. The District Line station was opened as HAMMERSMITH on 9 September 1874.

Hampstead in the 1920s. Heath Street is on the right.

Hampstead is a name of simple meaning being derived from Old English *ham*, 'a home' and *stede* 'a site' – meaning, literally 'the home-site', and probably refers to a farm-site. Recorded as *Hemstede* in the 10th century and *Hamstede* in the Domesday Book.

Prior to the station's opening the name Heath Street was proposed, but the station opened as HAMPSTEAD on 22 June 1907.

Hanger Lane was named *Hanger Hill* in 1710 and marks the site of a wood recorded as *le Hangrewode* in 1393 and is derived from the Old English *hangra* 'a wooded hill' with clinging steep slopes, later changed to *Lane*.

The station was opened as HANGER LANE on 30 June 1947.

Harlesden was recorded as *Herulvestune* in the Domesday Book and comes from the personal name of the Saxon *Heoruwulf* (or *Herewuff*) and Old English *tun*, 'a farm' – means 'Heoruwulf's farm', being on a site where he and his family once lived. It was recorded as *Herlesdon* in 1291.

The station was opened as HARLESDEN by the London & North Western Railway on 15 June 1912 and first used by Underground trains on 16 April 1917.

Harrow & Wealdstone – for *Harrow* see Harrow-on-the-Hill. *Wealdstone* was *Weald Stone* in 1754 and the name probably derives from the Old English *weald*, 'a forest', indicating that the land here was once covered by the heavy Middlesex woodlands, and a 'boundary stone'. A 'stone', three feet tall, still stands outside the 'Wealdstone Inn' but it is doubtful if this is the original one. We may assume that *Wealdstone* means 'the boundary stone in the forest'. The growth of this place dates from the opening of the London & Birmingham Railway.

The station was opened by the London & Birmingham Railway as HARROW on 20 July 1837. It was renamed HARROW & WEALDSTONE on 1 May 1897 and first used by Underground trains on 16 April 1917.

Harrow-on-the-Hill. The history of *Harrow* reminds us of the times before Christianity ousted paganism from England, for the name is derived from the Old English *hearg*, 'heathen temple or shrine'. *Harrow* is a prominent isolated hill rising about 300 feet above the Middlesex plain and here, perhaps on the site of the present church, must have stood a temple (or idol) of ancient heathen worship. It was recorded as *Hergas* in 832 and as *Herges* in the Domesday Book but had changed to *Harowe* by 1369.

An early twentieth century view of Station Road, Harrow.

There is an earlier name referring to *Gumeninga*; this may be a tribal people who were pagans, but nothing is really known. Harrow is famous for its public school.

The station was opened as Harrow on 2 August 1880, and renamed Harrow-on-the-Hill on 1 June 1894.

Hatton Cross was recorded as *Hatone* in 1230 and is derived from the Old English *haep*, 'heath' and *tun*, 'a farm' – and means 'the farm on the heath'. The cross may have some reference to an old boundary mark, but more convincingly a reference to the road junction.

The station was opened as Hatton Cross on 19 July 1975.

Heathrow (Terminals 1, 2, 3, Terminal 4 and Terminal 5). *Heathrow* was recorded as *Hetherewe* in 1547 and was, perhaps, the home of John atte *Hethe* who lived here in the 14th century. The name is probably derived from the Old English *haep*, 'heath' and *raew*,'row' – 'the row of houses on the heath'. Alternatively, the second half of the name may derive from the old English word *ruh* which means 'rough or uncultivated ground', and perhaps Heathrow originally was 'the rough heath'. It now houses one of the world's busiest airports.

Heathrow Terminals 1,2,3 was opened as Heathrow Central on 16 December 1976, which was changed to Heathrow Central Terminals 1,2,3 on 3 October 1983 and gained its present name on 12 April 1986. Heathrow Terminal 4 station was opened on 12 April 1986.

Heathrow Terminal 5, opening spring 2008, is the only Underground station owned by BAA, the airport company.

Hendon Central. *Hendon* was recorded as *Hendun* c.959 and as *Handone* in the Domesday Book. The name is derived from the Old English *haeh*, 'high' and *dun*, 'down or hill' – and means 'At the high hill', referring to the old village of *Hendon* clustered round the church of St Mary, atop a high hill.

The station opened as HENDON CENTRAL on 19 November 1923.

High Barnet was recorded as *Barneto* c.1070 and as *la Bernet* in 1235 and is derived from the Old English *baernet* – 'a place cleared by burning' – or '*bernette*', a French word for slope – i.e. Barnet Hill. Ground was cleared this way by early settlers. *High* refers to its geographical location.

The station was opened as HIGH BARNET by the Great Northern Railway on 1 April 1872 and first used by Underground trains on 14 April 1940.

Highbury & Islington. Originally *Highbury* was a summer camp of the Romans and during the 13th century the Priory of St John of Jerusalem had a manor here that was destroyed in 1381. Recorded as *Heybury* during the 14th century, the name is derived from *high* and the Old English *burh*, 'the manor on high ground', as opposed to nearby Canonbury and Barnsbury which stand on lower ground. *Islington*, recorded as *Gislandune* c.1000 and *Isendone* in the Domesday Book, is derived from: 1– the personal name *Gisla* and Old English *dun*, 'hill or down' – 'Gisla's hill' referring to a Saxon and his family who once lived on a site here, or; 2– the Old English *Gisel*, 'a hostage' and *dun*, 'hill' – indicating that hostages were once held here, or 3– Old English *Isel*, 'lower' and *don* – which can be interpreted as meaning 'a fortified enclosure'. It was recorded as *Islyndon* in 1554.

The station was opened as HIGHBURY on 28 June 1904 and renamed HIGHBURY & ISLINGTON on 20 July 1922.

Highgate. From very early times tolls were collected from travellers who used the Bishop of London's road across his park at Hornsey which then led to Finchley. This was at the *High Gate* (*Le Heghgate* recorded in 1354) which gave its name to the hamlet and later village at one of the highest points in London.

The station was opened as HIGHGATE by the Great Northern Railway on 22 August 1867, and first used by Underground trains on 19 January 1941. (See also *Archway*.)

High Street Kensington. For centuries two roads, both Roman in origin, one following the lines of the *High Street*, were the only means of east-west communication in this part of London. The first building in the vicinity took place during the reign of Charles II (1660–85) to the south of the present street, while the north side was built up during the 1780s. More development took place in the early 19th century, followed shortly afterwards by the arrival of the famous shops of the street.

Prior to the station's opening it was often referred to as KENSINGTON, but it was opened as HIGH STREET KENSINGTON on 1 October 1868. (See also *Kensington Olympia*.)

Hillingdon was recorded as *Hildendun* in 1078 and the name is derived from the personal name *Hilda* and the Old English *dun*, 'a hill' – and thus means 'Hilda's Hill' referring to a Saxon and her (or his – for Hilda may be a pet-name for *Hildwalf*) family who once lived here. It was recorded as *Hilendon* in 1254.

The station was opened as HILLINGDON on 10 December 1923.

Looking south down Kingsway in the late 1920s with the original Holborn Piccadilly Line station on the left. In the centre of the road can be seen the entrances to the tram subway station.

Holborn was recorded as *Holeburne* in 951 and takes its name from part of the River Fleet. It is derived from the Old English *holh*, 'a hollow' and *burna*, 'a stream' – means 'the stream (or brook) in the hollow'. The *hollow* is the valley now spanned by Holborn Viaduct. *Kingsway* is the street that runs from Holborn station to the Aldwych, and was begun in 1901 to clear the slums of this area. It was opened by Edward VII in 1905. There was some controversy over the choice of name but finally *Kingsway* was chosen, no doubt for patriotic reasons.

The station was opened as HOLBORN on 15 December 1906 for the Piccadilly Line. The Central Line platforms (replacing BRITISH MUSEUM station) were opened on 25 September 1933.

Holland Park. In the park is *Holland House*, a historic Jacobean mansion begun in 1605 and attributed to John Thorpe, which was originally called Cope's Castle as it was built for Sir Walter Cope. The House passed by marriage to Sir Henry Rich, who was created Earl of *Holland* in Lincolnshire in 1624, and who gave his name to the house and park. The whole estate was sold to the London County Council in 1952.

Prior to the station's opening the name of LANSDOWN ROAD was considered, but it opened as HOLLAND PARK on 30 July 1900.

Holloway Road station shortly after opening.

Holloway Road is a common road name and as it may suggest means 'the way in the hollow'; the road name later became the name of the district. The *hollow* refers to the fact that the hamlets of this area were situated on rather low-lying ground between Highgate and Islington; called *le Holeweye* in 1307.

Early plans show the station's name as plain HOLLOWAY, but it opened as HOLLOWAY ROAD on 15 December 1906.

Hornchurch. From ancient records there is a reference (in 1222) to the *horned church* (or monastery) in this district. Nothing of the monks' first church survives today, but the present building contains a bull's head and *horns* affixed to the east end, which has been here since at least 1610. The reason for this is rather obscure. It is possible that it could be a reference to a seal of a

French monastery or that it could be a reference to the tanning industry which once flourished in this area.

The station was opened as HORNCHURCH by the London, Tilbury & Southend Railway on 1 May 1885, and was first used by Underground trains on 2 June 1902.

Hounslow Central. *Hounslow* was recorded as *Honeslaw* in the Domesday Book and is derived from the Old English personal name *Hund* and *hlaw*, 'a hill' – means 'the hill where Hund lived'. It has no connection with dogs (unlike Houndsditch) as the name may suggest. It was recorded as *Hounslawe* in 1252.

The station was opened as HESTON HOUNSLOW on 1 April 1886; second station opened 19 October 1912; renamed HOUNSLOW CENTRAL 1 December 1925.

Hounslow East – see Hounslow Central.

The first station (on a spur line) was opened on 1 May 1883 as HOUNSLOW; renamed HOUNSLOW TOWN in 1884. It was closed on 31 March 1886; re-opened on 1 March 1903; and finally closed on 1 May 1909. A new station (on the main line) was opened on 2 May 1909 and renamed HOUNSLOW EAST 1 December 1925.

Hounslow West – see Hounslow Central.

The station was opened as HOUNSLOW BARRACKS 21 July 1884; renamed HOUNSLOW WEST 1 December 1925; new station opened 11 December 1926.

Hyde Park Corner. A name that occurs frequently both in the Domesday Book and in place-names is *hide*, which has been described as 'a piece of ground sufficiently large and fertile to maintain an ordinary household'. *Hyde Park* was named after a hide of land belonging to the Manor of Ebury, for at about the time of the Domesday Book the manor was divided into three smaller parts, one being called *Hyde*. From the time of the Norman Conquest until the Dissolution (1066–1536) the Hyde was in the possession of Westminster Abbey. It was then taken by Henry VIII and converted into a royal deer-park. In 1635 Charles I opened it to the public. The *Corner* was the entrance to London until 1825 when the turnpike was removed. It now consists of an open triangular space, enlarged in 1888 when a portion of nearby Green Park was taken for the roadway.

The station was opened as HYDE PARK CORNER on 15 December 1906.

I

Ickenham was recorded as *Ticheha* in the Domesday Book and is derived from the personal name of the Saxon *Ticea* (or *Ica*) and Old English *ham*, 'a home' – and means 'the home of Ica' and his family that once lived on a site here. Recorded as *Ikenham* in 1236.

The station was opened as ICKENHAM HALT 25 September 1905.

K

Kennington was recorded as *Chenintune* in the Domesday Book and is derived from the personal name of the Saxon *Cena* and Old English *tun*, 'a farm' – therefore it means 'the farm of Cena' an early inhabitant of the area. It was recorded as *Kenigton* in 1275.

Prior to the station's opening the name of NEW STREET was proposed, but it was opened as KENNINGTON on 18 December 1890.

Kensal Green was recorded as *Kingisholte* in 1255 and means the *King's Wood* (*King* and Old English *holt*, 'a wood') but just who the royal owner was is unknown. *The Green* is recorded in 1550 and lies just south of the station; it includes the Kensal Green Cemetery.

The station was opened as KENSAL GREEN on 1 October 1916.

Kensington Olympia is recorded as *Cheninton* in the Domesday Book and the name is derived from the personal name of the Saxon *Cynesige* and the Old English *tun*, 'a farm' – it means 'the farm of Cynesige', another local agriculturist. It has had many variant spellings, with *Kenesingeton* recorded in 1274. *Olympia* is the name of the huge exhibition building opened in 1886 and extended to the main road in 1930.

The station was opened by the West London Railway as KENSINGTON on 27 May 1844; re-sited farther north 2 June 1862; re-named KENSINGTON (ADDISON ROAD) in 1868; re-named KENSINGTON (OLYMPIA) 19 December 1946.

Kentish Town stands recorded as *Kentisston* in 1208 and the name seems to be derived from a farm held by someone nick-named *le Kentiss*(*h*) – and means *Kentish Farm*, but the real

Kilburn High Road in c.1906.

history of the name is, however, unknown. It was only coinci-
dence that Charles Pratt, Earl Camden, obtained through his
marriage the Manor of Kentish Town in 1791. He in fact took his
name from Camden Place in Kent. The *Town* developed in the
later part of the 18th century as an industrialised area of north
west London.

The station was opened as KENTISH TOWN on 22 June 1907.

Kenton was recorded as *Keninton* in 1232 and the name is
derived from the personal name of the Saxon *Coena* and the Old
English *tun*, 'a farm' – and means 'the farm of Coena' and his
family who once lived on a site here (see the similarity with
Kennington).

The station was opened as KENTON by the London & North
Western Railway on 15 June 1912 and first used by Underground
trains on 16 April 1917.

Kew Gardens – officially the Royal Botanic Gardens – were
founded in 1759 by Princess Augusta (mother of George III), in
the grounds of Kew House and Richmond Lodge. Kew House
was demolished in 1802. Noted for its great variety of plants
and wild-life, the gardens now cover 288 acres and were given to
the nation by Queen Victoria in 1841. *Kew* is the name of this
district on the south bank of the Thames and its name is derived
from the Middle English *Key* – meaning 'a quay or wharf'.

The station was opened as KEW GARDENS by the London & South Western Railway on 1 January 1869 and first used by Underground trains on 1 June 1877.

Kilburn, recorded as *Cuneburna* in 1121, takes its name from a stream which rose in Hampstead and flowed across West London, finally joining the River Thames near Chelsea Bridge. Only parts of the stream are in existence today and it has other names in different localities. Where it once turned south to Kilburn High Road it was known as the *Kylbourne* (1502). The name is derived from the Old English *cyne-burna*, 'royal stream' or 'cows' stream'. Although *Cylla* (a once local inhabitant of the area) has also been given as a possible derivation, the first definition seems correct.

The station was opened as KILBURN & BRONDESBURY on 24 November 1879; re-named KILBURN on 25 September 1950.

Kilburn Park – see Kilburn. The only remaining link with the Park today is the Kilburn Park Road to the south of the station.

The station was opened as KILBURN PARK on 31 January 1915.

Kingsbury was recorded as *Kynges byrig* in 1046 and as *Chingesberie* in the Domesday Book. The name is derived from *Kings* and the Old English *burh*, 'a fortified place' and means the 'King's manor or stronghold'. The manor was granted to Westminster Abbey by Edward the Confessor (reigned 1042-66) and the association of the area with a King goes back to at least 957, when the woodland in the parish was referred to as *Kings Wood*. It has had various spellings, being known as *Kyngesbury* in 1199.

The station was opened as KINGSBURY on 10 December 1932.

King's Cross St Pancras. The district of north London now known as *King's Cross* was originally called Battlebridge, traditionally the site of one of the battles between Boudicca (Boadicea), the British Queen of the Iceni, and the Romans about A.D. 59 or 61 at the bridge over the River Fleet. A corruption in the Cockney dialect of Bradeford ('broad ford' – over the Holborn or Fleet River) was recorded in 1207. Later, however, the district took its present name from a statue of King George IV which stood from 1830-45 at the crossroads here. This name was generally in use when the then Great Northern Railway adopted it for its terminus in 1850. *St Pancras* was once a solitary village and later a manor granted by Ethelbert (reigned 860-866) to St Paul's Cathedral. Recorded as *Sanctum Pancratiú* in the

The cut and cover method of building the Metropolitan Line shows the trench in the foreground with the completed tunnel beyond. On the is the clocktower of King's Cross Great Northern Railway station.

Domesday Book, the old village took its name from the church dedicated to the boy martyr *St Pancras* (*Pancratius*). According to tradition this site is one of the first near London on which a church was built, but now the old church (much restored) lies nearly forgotten behind the Midland Railway main-line station named after it, which was opened in 1868. Tradition has it that the station is situated on part of Cæsar's camp dating from c.BC50.

The Metropolitan Line station was opened on 10 January 1863 as KING'S CROSS; re-named KING'S CROSS & ST PANCRAS in 1925; KING'S CROSS FOR ST PANCRAS in 1927; and KING'S CROSS ST PANCRAS in 1933. It was replaced by a new station farther west on 14 March 1941; this new station was adjacent to the tube stations for the Piccadilly Line (which was opened on 15 December 1906) and the Northern Line (opened on 12 May 1907). Building the Victoria Line involved extensive reconstruction, the present station being brought into use on 1 December 1968.

Knightsbridge was recorded as *Cnihtebricge* in 1046 and can be interpreted as meaning 'the bridge of the young men'. It appears that these men were responsible for the upkeep or the defence of the bridge over the Westbourne stream where it crossed the Great West Road. The street has had many variant spellings and was known as *Knyghtesbrugg* 1364. One story has it that this was the place where knights had their jousting tournaments in days gone by, but this should be taken with that often used 'pinch of salt'. The stream still flows under Albert Gate, Knightsbridge, but is now buried deep in a sewer pipe.

On early plans the station's name was shown as SLOANE STREET, but it opened as KNIGHTSRIDGE on 15 December 1906.

L

Ladbroke Grove. Richard *Ladbrooke* owned the land here in 1624 and his family sold it for building purposes in 1845, giving their name to this long street running to the north of the station.

The station was opened as NOTTING HILL on 13 June 1864; re-named NOTTING HILL & LADBROKE GROVE 1880; re-named LADBROKE GROVE (NORTH KENSINGTON) on 1 June 1919; and LADBROKE GROVE in 1938.

Lambeth North. The name *Lambeth* is a reminder of the days when ships from all parts of the world sailed into the heart of London along the River Thames. Recorded in 1041 as *Lambhyo* and as *Lanchei* in the Domesday Book, it is derived from Old English *Lambe* and *hythe*, 'a haven' or 'port' – and means 'the port where lambs or cattle are shipped'. The suggestion that the first element of the name is from Old English *lam* 'dirt' or 'mud' can be discounted.

The station was opened as KENNINGTON ROAD on 10 March 1906; re-named WESTMINSTER BRIDGE ROAD on 5 August 1906; and LAMBETH NORTH on 15 April 1917.

Lancaster Gate is one of the gates into Hyde Park and could have received its name in honour of Queen Victoria, in her capacity as Duchess of Lancaster. A street of the same name, roughly opposite the gate, was built in 1863-66.

Prior to the station's opening the name of WESTBOURNE was proposed, but it opened as LANCASTER GATE on 30 July 1900.

Latimer Road. Edward *Latymer*, who died in 1626, bequeathed the land either side of the road to support the scholars of Latymer school in which he took an interest. The road runs north

Ladbroke Grove before the days of heavy motor traffic.

west of the station and ran closer to it prior to the building of Westway. What remains of its southern half is now named Freston Road.

The station opened as LATIMER ROAD on 16 December 1868.

Leicester Square. In 1631 Robert Sidney, 2nd Earl of *Leicester*, later British Ambassador to France (1636–41), obtained a licence to build his London residence here at a place then known as *Lammas Land*. The square, which takes its name from the Earl, was laid out in 1665, being called *Leicester Fields* and later *Square*, being converted to a public garden in 1874. *Leicester House* was built on the north side in 1637, pulled down in 1790, rebuilt in the early 19th century and destroyed by fire in 1865.

On early plans the station's name was shown as CRANBOURN STREET, but it opened as LEICESTER SQUARE on 15 December 1906.

Leyton was recorded as *Lugetune* c.1050 and *Leyton* in 1226. It is derived from *Lea* (the river) and the Old English *tun*, 'a farm' – and thus means 'the farm on the River Lea'. *Lea* is a Celtic name possibly meaning 'light river' or 'sparkling stream'.

The station was opened as LOW LEYTON by the Eastern Counties Railway on 22 August 1856; re-named LEYTON on 1 January 1868. It was first used by Underground trains on 5 May 1947.

Leytonstone has the same meaning as Leyton with the addition of the word ending, *stone*. Recorded as Leyton *at(te) Stone* in 1370, tradition explains that this spot is near Leyton and the High *Stone*, a boundary mark.

The station was opened as LEYTONSTONE by the Eastern Counties Railway on 22 August 1856 and was first used by Underground trains on 5 May 1947.

Liverpool Street. In 1246, on the site now occupied by the station, a priory was erected (later to become the *Bethlehem Hospital*) which stood here until 1676 when it was removed to London Wall. In 1829 the street was widened and named in honour of Lord *Liverpool*, who was Prime Minister from 1812–1827. The whole area was cleared after 1864 for the building and opening for local traffic of the *Liverpool Street* main-line station of the Great Eastern Railway in 1874. Metropolitan Line trains ran into it between 1 February and 11 July 1875.

The Metropolitan Railway station was opened as BISHOPSGATE on 12 July 1875 and re-named LIVERPOOL STREET on 1 November 1909. The Central Line reached Liverpool Street on 28 July 1912.

This was how Liverpool Street terminus of the Great Eastern Railway looked in about 1912 when the Central London Railway tube was opening its own deep level terminus. To the left is the North London Railway's Broad Street terminus.

London Bridge. It is possible that there was a bridge not far east of the present one in the year 43 and there have been many bridges across the River Thames here in the course of history, the fifth and latest one being opened in March 1973 and the old bridge being sold and re-erected stone by stone in Arizona. The poem which opens 'London Bridge is falling down' refers to the Battle in 1014 between King Aethelred of the English and the Danes, after which the bridge collapsed. *London* recorded as Londinium c.115 is a Celtic place-name probably formed from a personal name *Londinos* – meaning 'the bold one'.

The Underground station was opened as LONDON BRIDGE on 25 February 1900.

Loughton, recorded as *Lukintone* in 1062 and as *Lochetuna* in the Domesday Book, is derived from the personal name of the Saxon *Luhha* (or *Luea*) and Old English *tun*, 'a farm' – it means 'the farm of Luhha', an early local Essex inhabitant.

The original station was opened as LOUGHTON by the Eastern Counties Railway on 22 August 1856. It was re-sited on 24 April 1865. A new station was opened on 28 April 1940 in readiness for Underground trains, which took over the service from British Railways (Eastern Region) on 21 November 1948.

M

Maida Vale, though used as the name of a district, is really only a street name. It takes its name from *Maida*, a town in Calabria, Italy, where Sir John Stuart defeated the French in 1806. The street was mentioned in 1868, runs north to south and is, in fact, part of the Edgware Road.

Prior to the station's opening the name of ELGIN AVENUE was proposed, but it opened as MAIDA VALE on 6 June 1915.

Manor House. Close by the station stands the *Manor House* public house. Known as the 'Manor Tavern' when it was built in c.1820 as a stopping place for travellers between London and Cambridge, it was re-named in 1931 after a *manor house* situated opposite. At this time the public house was rebuilt and the house demolished to make way for St Olave's Church.

The station was opened as MANOR HOUSE on 19 September 1932.

In its first six years before the start of the Second World War, London Transport built with even more ferocity upon the civic pride it had inherited. This was a combined sign at Manor House for the Underground, directional sign for road users and post for supporting the overhead electrical wiring to feed the trams.

Mansion House has been the official residence of the Lord Mayor of London since 1753. The house was designed by George Dance and built in 1739-53 on the site of the old Stocks market and St Mary Woolchurch. The building received some damage in the Second World War. The City Police Court is in the same building.

The station was erected on the site of the Church of Holy Trinity the Less and later a Lutheran church.

The station was opened as MANSION HOUSE on 3 July 1871.

The view down Oxford Street from the junction with Edgware Road has hardly changed since this photo of Marble Arch was taken in the mid-1930s.

Marble Arch was designed by Nash more or less after the 'Arch of Constantine' in Rome and the building was originally erected in 1828 in front of Buckingham Palace. It was removed in 1850–51 to its present site where it was an entrance to Hyde Park until 1908. The arch is constructed of Carrara *marble*.

The station was opened as MARBLE ARCH on 30 July 1900.

Marylebone. Local feeling with regard to place names should always be taken into consideration, for there is a story regarding how *Marylebone* received its name. For countless years the place had been known as *Tyburn* (*Tiburne* in the Domesday Book) but the association with the tragic tree became too grim and so the local folk took a new name for their parish, being a dedication of the local Church of *St Mary-by-the-Bourn*, thus 'Tyburn' became *Maryburne* and is so recorded in 1453. The *le* (by or near) was added later, the district being known as *Mary le bone* in 1746. Tyburn survived until the end of the 18th century in the *Tyburn Tree*, an execution place, near the present Marble Arch.

During the station's planning it was referred to as either MARYLEBONE or LISSON GROVE (where the entrance then was), but it opened as GREAT CENTRAL (reflecting the ownership of the adjacent main line station) on 27 March 1907; re-named MARYLEBONE 15 April 1917.

Mile End was recorded as *La Mile ende* in 1288. The then hamlet was so named because of its position on the old London – Colchester road at a distance of about *one mile* from Aldgate.

The station was opened as Mile End on 2 June 1902. It was rebuilt and re-opened 4 December 1946.

Mill Hill East. Mill Hill was recorded as *Myllehill* in 1547 and as the name suggests means 'the mill on the hill'. The original site, *Mill Field*, lies to the north of the present *Mill Hill* village but there is no evidence that a mill ever existed.

The station was opened as Mill Hill by the Great Northern Railway on 22 August 1867; re-named Mill Hill East on 1 March 1928. In readiness for its use by Underground trains, the committee of the New Works Programme 1935/40 suggested that a change of name to Bittacy Hill might avoid confusion with other Mill Hill stations. However Mill Hill East remained when the station was first used by Underground trains on 18 May 1941 mainly to serve the nearby barracks.

Monument. This well-known London landmark was erected during the 1670s and is a hollow column 202 feet high designed by Sir Christopher Wren and Robert Hooke. It commemorates the Great Fire of London in 1666 and the height of the monument is said to be the exact distance from the baker's shop in nearby Pudding Lane where the fire started.

Prior to the station's opening it was, for a time, referred to as King William Street, but it was opened as Eastcheap on 6 October 1884 and re-named Monument on 1 November 1884.

Moorgate station soon after opening in 1865.

MOORGATE-STREET STATION OF THE METROPOLITAN RAILWAY.

Moorgate. As the name suggests this was the site of one of the *gates* in the old City wall. The first *Moor gate* was cut into the wall in 1415 to give access to the moorland lying to the north of London. As the wall crumbled during the 18th century the gate was demolished in 1760. The thoroughfare called *Moorgate* was built in 1846 and, in fact, runs from the site of the old gate.

The *moor* itself was virtually uninhabited and remained un-used throughout the Middle Ages except by crowds of ice skaters who gathered in the winter months. As the area was built up over the years, The Moorfields became London's first civic park and today places such as Finsbury Square and Finsbury Circus are part of the original Moor.

The station was opened as MOORGATE STREET on 23 December 1865 and re-named MOORGATE on 24 October 1924. The Northern Line station, always called MOORGATE, was opened on 25 February 1900.

Moor Park was recorded as *la More* c.1180 and the meaning is self-explanatory. The original site of the settlement was evidently a *Moor Farm* which once stood in the River Colne water meadows, near a tract of marshy land.

The station was opened as SANDY LODGE on 9 May 1910; re-named MOOR PARK & SANDY LODGE on 18 October 1923 and MOOR PARK on 25 September 1950.

Morden was recorded as *Mordone* in the Domesday Book and the name is derived from Old English *mor*, 'a marsh' and *dun*, 'a hill' – it means 'marshy hill' but the interpretation 'hill in the fens' seems more correct. *Morden* occupies a hill overlooking lower ground.

Before the station opened, the name NORTH MORDEN was proposed, but it opened as MORDEN on 13 September 1926.

Mornington Crescent was begun in 1821 by Ferdinand, the second Lord Southampton, and is named after a famous connection of the family. For the Lord's sister-in-law was Anne Wellesley, whose maiden name was *Mornington*, being the daughter of the Earl of Mornington and sister of the Duke of Wellington.

Prior to the station's opening the name of SEYMOUR STREET was proposed, but it was opened as MORNINGTON CRESCENT on 22 June 1907. It was closed – originally intended to be permanently – on 23 October 1992, but re-opened following refurbishment on 27 April 1998.

N

Neasden was recorded as *Neasdun* in 939 and the name is derived from the Old English *naess*, 'nose' and *dun*, 'hill' – it means 'the nose-shaped hill' referring to a well defined landmark of this area. It was known as *Needsden* in 1750, and the present spelling appeared at a later date.

The station was opened as KINGSBURY & NEASDEN on 2 August 1880; re-named NEASDEN & KINGSBURY on 1 January 1910 and NEASDEN on 1 January 1932.

Newbury Park was recorded in 1348 and is derived from *new* and Old English *burh*, 'manor house'. It therefore means 'the (then) new manor', in the *park*.

The station was opened as NEWBURY PARK by the Great Eastern Railway on 1 May 1903 and was first used by Underground trains on 14 December 1947.

North Acton – see Acton Town.

The station was opened as NORTH ACTON on 5 November 1923. (There had been a Great Western Railway halt named North Acton, to the west of the present station, from 2 May 1904 to 31 January 1913).

North Ealing – see Ealing Broadway.

The station was opened as NORTH EALING on 23 June 1903.

The station at North Ealing retains its original District Railway building. It has been served by the Piccadilly Line since 1932.

Northfields station when still part of the District Railway and before rebuilding.

Northfields is a new district name preserving the old field-name *Northfield* which is self-explanatory, being recorded in 1455.

The station was opened as NORTHFIELD HALT on 16 April 1908; re-named NORTHFIELDS & LITTLE EALING 11 December 1911; re-sited as NORTHFIELDS, east of the old site, on 19 May 1932.

North Harrow – see Harrow-on-the-Hill.

The station was opened as NORTH HARROW on 22 March 1915.

North Greenwich. Greenwich it seems was given its name by either the Saxon invaders of the sixth century who called it *Green Village* – from the Old English *green* and *wic*. Or maybe the invading Danes of the ninth century who called it the 'Green Reach', the reach referring to the straight part of the River Thames on which Greenwich stands. It was recorded as *Grenewc* in 964 and *Grenvtz* in the Domesday Book (1086). The place of course is famous for being on '0 degrees' of longtitude and therefore 'Standard Time' for most countries of the World is based on 'Greenwich Time'.

The station was opened as NORTH GREENWICH on 14 May 1999.

Northolt was recorded as *nord healum* in 960 and as *Northala* in the Domesday Book and the name is derived from the Old English *nord*, 'north' and *health*, 'heath' – it means 'the north heath' or 'angle of land' in contrast to Southall. Known as *Northolt* by 1610.

The station was opened for Underground trains as NORTHOLT on 21 November 1948, replacing a halt of the same name, but on a different site, which had been opened by the GWR on 1 May 1907.

North Wembley – see Wembley Central.

The station was opened as WEMBLEY CENTRAL by the London & North Western Railway on 15 June 1912, and was first used by Underground trains on 16 April 1917.

Northwick Park is a modern name and comes from the *Northwick* family, Lords of the Manor of Harrow in 1797.

The station was opened as NORTHWICK PARK & KENTON on 28 June 1923; re-named NORTHWICK PARK, 15 March 1937.

Northwood was recorded as *Northwode* in 1435 and was originally the name of a *Wood* and farm lying to the *north* of Ruislip. The present town dates chiefly from the construction of the railway c.1885.

The station was opened as NORTHWOOD on 1 September 1887.

Northwood Hills – see Northwood. The Hills refer to nearby high ground. The station may have received its name as a result of a public competition sponsored by the Metropolitan Railway.

The station opened as NORTHWOOD HILLS on 13 November 1933.

Notting Hill Gate was recorded as *Knottynghull* in 1356 but the origin of the name is in some doubt. It may be taken from the Old English *cnotting*, 'a hill', or more probably it is the name (or nickname) for a family who settled in this area in early times, called *Knottying*. Recorded as *Noding Hill* in 1680 and with the present spelling at a later date. A gate formerly stood at the junction of Kensington Church Street and the main road and was removed in 1864.

The station was opened as NOTTING HILL GATE on 1 October 1868.

Notting Hill Gate, with the original Central London Railway station building on the right. The station was completely rebuilt in 1959/60.

O

Oakwood takes its name from the nearby *Oakwood Park*, or possibly a large house which once stood here called *Oak Lodge*.

The names of EAST BARNET and MERRYHILLS were considered but the station was opened as ENFIELD WEST on 13 March 1933; re-named ENFIELD WEST (OAKWOOD) ON 3 May 1934, and OAKWOOD on 1 September 1946.

Old Street was recorded as *Ealdestrate* c.1200 and *le Oldestrete* in 1373. Originally a Roman Road, then the old highway from the Aldersgate to the north-east of England, before Bishopsgate was built.

The station was opened as OLD STREET on 17 November 1901.

Olympia – see Kensington (Olympia)

Osterley was recorded as *Osterle* in 1274 and the name is derived from either the Old English word *eowestre*, which can be interpreted as meaning 'sheepfold clearing', being once pasture land, or Old English *ost*, 'a knob of land' and *leah*, 'a glade', which can be interpreted as meaning 'a hillock'. Recorded as *Austerley* 1609 and *Osterley* at a later date.

The station was opened as OSTERLEY & SPRING GROVE on 1 May 1883. It was re-sited further west and the new station opened on 25 March 1934 as OSTERLEY. The earlier station can still be seen.

Oval is the famous ground of the Surrey County Cricket Club which was formed in 1884, the name *Oval* coming from the shape of the ground. The first piece of turf was laid in March 1845. The first cricket match was played on or about 13 May of that year, and the first Test match in England (*v.* Australia) in 1880.

Prior to the station's opening the name of KENNINGTON OVAL was considered, and may have been used for a short time after opening. Officially, the station was opened as OVAL on 18 December 1890.

Oxford Circus takes its name from *Oxford Street* of which it forms a part. This was the old road to *Oxford* in 1682, recorded as Oxford Road in 1720, and Oxford Street in 1725. The *Circus* was originally named Regent Circus until the late 19th century.

The station was opened as OXFORD CIRCUS on 30 July 1900.

P

Paddington was recorded as *Padintune* in 959 and the name is derived from the personal name of the Saxon *Padda* and the Old English *tun*, 'a farm – it means 'the farm of Padda', an Anglo Saxon chieftain. Recorded as *Patyngton* in 1398 and changed to *Paddington* in the course of time.

The Circle Line station (opposite The Great Western Station Hotel) was opened as PADDINGTON (PRAED STREET) on 1 October 1868; re-named PADDINGTON 11 July 1948. The Hammersmith & City Line station (alongside the main line platform 12) was opened as PADDINGTON (BISHOP'S ROAD) on 10 January 1863; re-named PADDINGTON on 10 September 1933. The Bakerloo Line station was opened as PADDINGTON on 1 December 1913.

Park Royal was the grand name given to a piece of land where an unsuccessful attempt was made to establish a fixed ground for the Royal Agricultural Society Annual Show. Before the First World War the land was built over and the name became that of a district.

The station was opened as PARK ROYAL & TWYFORD ABBEY on 23 June 1903; re-sited 6 July 1931 and re-named PARK ROYAL.

Parsons Green. As the name suggests, this was the hamlet which grew up round the *parsonage* house of Fulham, being

Piccadilly Circus in the 19th century looking up Regent Street.

recorded as *Personesgrene* in 1391. The *Green* is now a small triangular piece of land on the edge of which stands the parish church.

The station was opened as PARSONS GREEN on 1 March 1880.

Perivale. This district was originally known as Greneford and is recorded as this in the Domesday Book, later to be known as Little Greenford (in 1386) a distinction from Greenford (or Great Greenford). The name was changed by 1508 to *Pyryvale* and is derived from Middle English *perie*, 'pear tree' and Old French *val*, 'vale' and means 'the valley with the pear trees', which referred to a nearby meadow. Called *Purevale* in the late 16th century, it changed to the present spelling in the course of time.

The station was opened for Underground trains as PERIVALE on 30 June 1947. It replaced a PERIVALE HALT on the Great Western Railway opened on 2 May 1904.

Piccadilly Circus. The name *Piccadilly* is probably derived from *Pickadilly Hall*, the popular name of a house built in c.1611 near Windmill Street by a retired tailor, Robert Baker, who made much of his fortune by the sale of 'pickadillies', a form of collar or ruff. The street was known as *Portugal Street* in 1692 in honour of Catharine of Braganza, the Queen of Charles II, but changed to *Pickadilly Street* by 1763. *The Circus*, built during the 19th century, covers the site of a house and garden belonging to a Lady Hutton; the garden was near a field known as the Round Ringill.

The station was opened as PICCADILLY CIRCUS on 10 March 1906. An extensively reconstructed station was opened on 10 December 1928.

Pimlico is a comparatively new district of London, recorded as *Pimplico* in 1630. It seems that the name was copied from a garden of public entertainment in Hoxton (north London), named after its owner, a well known inn-keeper, Ben *Pimlico*, whose name was also given to his inn (late 16th-century). There was once a *Pimlico Walk* in Hoxton. *Pimlico*, on the north bank of the Thames, was almost uninhabited before the 19th century.

The station was opened as PIMLICO on 14 September 1972.

Pinner was recorded as *Pinnora* in 1232 and the name is derived from a personal name (or nickname) *Pin* (or *Pinna*), and the Old English *ora*, 'bank edge' or Slope' – this refers to the original village street which slopes steeply up to the church from the Pinn River – and thus means 'the slope to Pinna's place'. It is

Pinner High Street about 100 years ago. Little has changed to its general appearance since this picture was taken.

certain that the River *Pinn* takes its name from the old village and not vice versa. It was recorded as *Pynnor* in 1483.

The station was opened as PINNER on 25 May 1885.

Plaistow was recorded as *Plagestoue* c.1200 and was the ancient site of a Manor and a place of court meetings. It was also, on occasions, the place where 'miracle plays' and similar entertainments were performed. The name is derived from the Old English *pleg*, 'sports' or 'playing' and *stowe*, 'place' – and means, simply, 'the playing-place'.

The station was opened as PLAISTOW by the London, Tilbury & Southend Railway on 31 March 1858; first used by Underground trains on 2 June 1902.

Preston Road was mentioned as *Preston* in 1194 and the name comes from the Old English *preast*, 'priest' and *tun* 'farm' – and means 'the farm belonging to the priest(s)'. A priest is mentioned in the Domesday Book as holding land in the parish of Harrow, possibly at this location. The *road* was added to the name as the district grew in the course of time.

The station was opened as PRESTON ROAD halt on 21 May 1908; new station (resited) 22 November 1931.

Putney Bridge was recorded as *Putelei* in the Domesday Book and the name is derived from the Saxon personal name *Puttan* and Old English *hyp*, 'a landing place' – 'Puttan's wharf. This was one of many such landing places on the River Thames. The original wooden *bridge* was erected in 1729 and replaced by the present stone bridge in 1884-86. It was widened in 1933.

The station was opened on 1 March 1880 as PUTNEY BRIDGE & FULHAM; re-named PUTNEY BRIDGE & HURLINGHAM 1 September 1902; PUTNEY BRIDGE 1932.

Queensbury really means 'a fortified place' but do not look for the remains in this part of north-west London. When the new Metropolitan Line to Stanmore was opened on 10 December 1932, one station was called Kingsbury. Two years later, a further station was opened and the name *Queensbury* was invented for it.

The station was opened as QUEENSBURY on 16 December 1934.

Queen's Park was the name adopted for a housing estate by the park that was built from the late 1870s onwards. It was so named in honour of Queen Victoria.

The original London & North Western Railway station was opened as QUEEN'S PARK (WEST KILBURN) on 2 June 1879. The present station was opened as QUEEN'S PARK for Underground trains on 11 February 1915.

Queensway, formerly called Black Line Lane, was named from the Public House once on the corner of the street. It was re-named in honour of *Queen* Victoria soon after she came to the throne in 1837. It is suggested that the reason was that, as a child, this was the place of Victoria's favourite horse ride; she then lived only half a mile away at Kensington Palace. It was at first called *Queen's Road*, then *Queensway* from January 1938.

The station was opened as QUEEN'S ROAD on 30 July 1900; re-named QUEENSWAY 1 September 1946.

Queensbury station before the Second World War.

R

Ravenscourt Park was the manor granted to Alice Perrers, the notorious favourite of Edward III (reigned 1327-77). It was known as Palyngewyk in 1270 (later Padingwick) and in 1819 a *Raven's Court House* was recorded in the area, but the history of this modern name is unknown. The Park lies opposite the station along Paddenswick Road.

The station was opened as SHAFTESBURY ROAD by the London & South Western Railway on 1 April 1873. It was re-named RAVENSCOURT PARK on 1 March 1888. First used by Underground trains on 1 June 1877.

Rayners Lane was developed as a suburban residential area in the 1930s. The lane is named after Daniel Rayner, who owned a farm on it during the early days of the Metropolitan Railway.

The station opened as RAYNERS LANE HALT on 26 May 1906.

Redbridge takes its name from the *bridge* over the River Roding on what is now the Eastern Avenue just outside Wanstead. The old *red bridge*, first recorded on a map in 1746, was probably a century older; it has been replaced by a more modern one but the original bridge has given a name to a whole new London borough.

Prior to the opening of the station two other names, ILFORD WEST and RED HOUSE, were considered, but it opened as REDBRIDGE on 14 December 1947.

Regent's Park station has never had a street level building. Ornate signs were erected at the heads of both sets of stairs from street to booking hall area.

Regent's Park, once Marylebone Park, was a Royal Hunting ground until the Interregnum, 1649. It reverted to the Crown in 1811 and was laid out afresh from 1812 onwards by John Nash for the Prince *Regent*, after whom it is named. At the same time Nash designed and built Regent Street as part of the 'Royal Mile' connecting the park with the Prince's house in St James's. Roughly circular in shape, the Park covers an area of 472 acres and includes the famous London Zoo.

The station was opened as REGENT'S PARK on 10 March 1906.

Richmond was known as Shene (meaning Shelter) from c.950 until 1502, when Henry VIII rebuilt the palace here after it had been burnt down by fire a year earlier. He called it *Richmond* (or *Richemount*) after his earldom so named in Yorkshire. This, in its turn, originally came from a name of a place in France. So modern *Richmond* obtained its name in a roundabout way.

The original London & South Western Railway station was opened as RICHMOND on 27 July 1846. The terminal station platforms were opened by the LSWR for the use of their own service from Hammersmith on 1 January 1869 and North London Railway trains from Broad Street. District Railway trains began on 1 June 1877 and the Metropolitan Railway served it between 1 October 1877 and 31 December 1906.

Rickmansworth was recorded as *Prichemareworde* in the Domesday Book and the name is derived from a personal name *Ricmaer* and Old English *worp*, 'enclosure' – and means 'Ricmaer's farm with the enclosure'. It seems that *Ricmaer* is a continental name and this person had recently come from Europe and settled here. There have been many changes of spelling including *Rikmersworth* in 1430, until the present spelling was adopted.

The station opened as RICKMANSWORTH on 1 September 1887.

Roding Valley takes its name from the River *Roding*. The river, however, took its name from the villages called *Reding* (or *Roothing*), which in turn came from the settlement of the people known as the *Hroda*, and was corrupted to *Roding* in the course of time. It was recorded as *duae Rotinges* in the 11th century and as *Rodon* in 1576. *The Valley* as such is no more than a shallow dip at this point.

The station was opened by the London & North Eastern Railway as RODING VALLEY on 3 February 1936 and was first used by Underground trains on 21 November 1948.

Royal Oak was the name of an old rural tavern, the entrance to which was by way of a wooden plank over the Westbourne River. This has now been replaced by the 'Railway Tap' public house which contains much of interest for any railway enthusiast. The station and district now take their name from the old tavern.

The station was opened as ROYAL OAK on 30 October 1871.

Ruislip was recorded as *Rislepe* in the Domesday Book and the name has one of London's most curious origins derived from Old English *ryse*, 'rush' and *hlype*, 'leap'. It seems to refer to a spot where the little River Pinn could once be crossed. It has had various spellings until recorded as *Ruislip* in 1527.

The station was opened as RUISLIP on 4 July 1904.

Ruislip Gardens – see Ruislip. The *Gardens* were taken from the name of a nearby 1930s housing development.

The station opened as RUISLIP GARDENS on 21 November 1948.

Ruislip Manor – see Ruislip. Today near the River Pinn lies *Manor* farm. This, and its surroundings, once held a priory dependent on the Norman Abbey of Bec. During the wars with France the Manor was confiscated by the Crown and the priory was closed in 1414. The land was granted to the Earl of Bedford, then to King's College, Cambridge, who still own the lordship of the manor.

The station opened as RUISLIP MANOR HALT on 5 August 1912.

Russell Square was named in 1800 by an Act of Parliament and was built between 1801-05. It takes its name from the Dukes of Bedford whose family name is *Russell*; they acquired lands in London in 1552 and later by marriage in 1669. The square was once part of an area known as Southampton Fields and later called Long Fields. The square was badly damaged during the Second World War, but has been redeveloped since to become the second largest square in London.

The station opened as RUSSELL SQUARE on 15 December 1906.

S

St James's Park lies on the site of an ancient hospital dedicated to *St James the Less*, from which it takes its name. It was part of a swamp until, on the orders of Henry VIII in 1532, it was drained to become a bowling green, tilt yard, and breeding ground for deer. John Nash re-designed the park in 1827–29.

The station was opened as ST JAMES'S PARK on 24 December 1868.

St John's Wood was recorded as *Sci Johannis* in 1294, and the *wood* was granted to the Knights Templars of St John of Jerusalem but later passed into the possession of the Hospitallers of this Order. This fashionable district of north-west London was first recorded as (*Grete*) *St John's Wood* in 1558.

The Metropolitan Railway station opened as ST JOHN'S WOOD ROAD on 13 April 1868; re-named ST JOHN'S WOOD on 1 April 1925; and further re-named LORDS on 11 June 1939. It was replaced together with MARLBOROUGH ROAD by a new St John's Wood station on the Bakerloo Line which opened on 20 November 1939. The new station was sited between the two closed stations and was originally planned to be named ACACIA ROAD.

St Paul's takes its name from the nearby Cathedral of the Diocese of London. The tradition that a Roman temple once stood here has no evidence to support it. There was, however, a Christian Church built here in the 7th century which was destroyed by fire in 1087. This is the third Cathedral built on the present site, and was planned by Sir Christopher Wren after the previous one had been destroyed in the Great Fire of London in 1666. Construction commenced in 1675 and was completed some 27 years later.

The station was originally to be named NEWGATE STREET, but opened as POST OFFICE on 30 July 1900, the General Post Office headquarters being close by. The station was re-named ST PAUL'S on 1 February 1937.

Seven Sisters took its name from *seven* elm trees which stood near Page Green, where the Seven Sisters Road (built 1831–33) joined the old Ermine Street. They were marked as *7 Sesters* in 1754, then *Seven Sisters* in 1805.

The station opened as SEVEN SISTERS on 1 September 1968.

Shepherd's Bush either takes its name from the *shepherds* who used this place as a meadow or more likely from a personal name of someone so called. It was recorded as *Sheppards Bush Green* in 1635.

The Central London Railway Shepherd's Bush Station was opened on 30 July 1900.

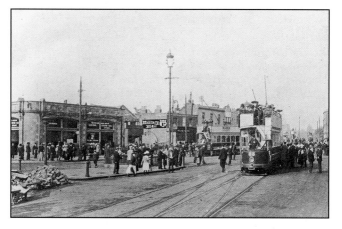

Shepherd's Bush soon after the arrival of the tube in 1900 and electric trams in 1901.

Shepherd's Bush Market - see Shepherd's Bush. The market is on Underground-owned land and opened for business in 1914 when the station was resited on the north side of the Uxbridge Road. The original station opened as Shepherd's Bush on 13 June 1864, being renamed on 12 October 2008.

Sloane Square. Like many other street names in this part of London, the square is named in honour of Sir Hans *Sloane* (1660–1753) the physician and botanist who purchased the manor of Chelsea from the Cheyne family in 1712. In 1749 his great collection of books and curiosities formed the basis of the British Museum. Over the station, through a square iron conduit 15 feet above the platforms, passes the River Westbourne which eventually reaches the River Thames by Chelsea Bridge.

The station was opened as SLOANE SQUARE on 24 December 1868. It was severely damaged in an air raid on 12 November 1940; rebuilding after the Second World War was completed on 3 May 1951.

Sloane Square station at the end of the 19th century.

Snaresbrook was so named in 1599 and takes its name from a nearby natural landmark. The name is derived from the Old English *shear*, 'swift' and *brook* – 'the swift flowing brook'.

The station was built as SNARESBROOK & WANSTEAD by the Eastern Counties Railway and opened on 22 August 1856. First used by Underground trains and re-named SNARESBROOK on 14 December 1947.

South Ealing – see Ealing Broadway.

The station was opened as SOUTH EALING on 1 May 1883.

Southfields was recorded as *Suthfield* in 1247 and takes its name from a great *field* where farm produce was once sold.

The station was opened as SOUTHFIELDS on 3 June 1889.

Southgate was so recorded in 1370 and was known as *le Southgate* in 1608. The hamlet here grew up at the *south gate* of Enfield Chase and is so named.

The name of CHASE SIDE was considered but the station was opened as SOUTHGATE on 13 March 1933.

South Harrow – see Harrow-on-the-Hill.

The station was opened as SOUTH HARROW on 28 June 1903. It was re-sited on 5 July 1935.

South Kensington – see Kensington.

Prior to the station's opening the name CROMWELL ROAD was considered, but it opened as SOUTH KENSINGTON on 24 December 1868, the Piccadilly Line tube station on 8 January 1907.

South Kenton – see Kenton.

The station was opened as SOUTH KENTON on 3 July 1933.

South Ruislip – see Ruislip.

The station was opened on 21 November 1948. The station on the adjacent main line was opened by the Great Western & Great Central Joint Committee as NORTHOLT JUNCTION on 1 May 1908. It was re-named SOUTH RUISLIP & NORTHOLT JUNCTION on 12 September 1932, and became SOUTH RUISLIP on 30 June 1947.

Southwark lies on the south side of the Thames. A stone bridge was built here over the river, probably by the Romans soon after they landed in AD43. Called *Suthriganawoerc* in the 10th century – meaning *'fort of the men of Surrey'*. It was recorded as *Sudwerca* in the Domesday Book – meaning *'southern defensive work or fort'*, from the Old English *suth* and *weorc*.

The station opened as SOUTHWARK on 20 November 1999.

South Wimbledon – see Wimbledon.

During planning of the station the name MERTON GROVE was used, but it was opened as SOUTH WIMBLEDON on 13 September 1926 as it was thought advantageous to the Underground to show the station's near connection to the somewhat better known Wimbledon.

South Woodford – see Woodford.

The station was opened as GEORGE LANE on 22 August 1856 by the Eastern Counties Railway. It was re-named SOUTH WOODFORD (GEORGE LANE) on 5 July 1937, and SOUTH WOODFORD in 1950. First used by Underground trains on 14 December 1947.

Stamford Brook was recorded in 1650 and this was the name of the stream which divided, near its mouth to the west, the parishes of Acton and Chiswick from Fulham, and further north was spanned by Bollo Bridge. The name is derived from a *stony ford*, once located here, where the main Great West Road crossed the stream.

The station opened as STAMFORD BROOK on 1 February 1912.

Stanmore was recorded *Stanmere* in the Domesday Book and is derived from the Old English *stan*, 'stony' and *mere*, 'a pool'. There are outcrops of gravel on the clay soil here and the *mere* may have been one of the ponds which still exist. Known as *Stanmore the Great* in 1574 – 'the Great' distinguished it from Whitchurch or Little Stanmore.

The station was opened as STANMORE on 10 December 1932.

Stepney Green. Stepney was recorded as *Stybbanhype* c.1000 and as *Stibenhede* in the Domesday Book and the name is derived from the Saxon personal name *Stebbing* and Old English *hyo*, 'hithe' or 'landing place'. It has had various spellings in the course of time until recorded as *Stepney* in 1534. *The Green* is now a street and was the home of John atte *Grene*.

The station was opened as STEPNEY GREEN on 23 June 1902.

Stockwell was recorded as *Stokewell* in 1188 and can be interpreted as meaning – 'the stream with a footbridge consisting of a tree trunk', referring to a natural location, which was once nearby. Derived from Old English – *stock* (trunk) and *wella* (stream), Stockwell was a small rural village until the 1860s.

The station was opened as STOCKWELL on 18 December 1890.

In the early 20th century Stratford was a thriving community with many of its local inhabitants employed at the Great Eastern Railway's main works.

Stonebridge Park. Where the Harrow Road crosses the River Brent stood a *stone bridge*, first recorded in 1745, that now gives its name to the district. It was recorded in 1875 that there was a cluster of 60 or 80 villas on a nearby estate which was given the name *Stonebridge Park*.

The station was opened as STONEBRIDGE PARK by the London & North Western Railway on 15 June 1912 and first used by Underground trains on 16 April 1917.

Stratford was recorded in 1177 and is derived from the Old English *straet*, 'road' and *ford* – and means 'the road with a ford'. The ford was where the Roman road to Colchester crossed one of the various branches of the River Lea.

The station was opened as STRATFORD on 4 December 1946. (The original Eastern Counties Railway station was opened on 20 June 1839.)

Sudbury Hill – see Sudbury Town. The Hill is the high ground to the north of Sudbury.

The station was opened as SUDBURY HILL on 28 June 1903.

Sudbury Town was recorded as *Suthbury* in 1282 and the name is derived from *south* and Old English *burh*, 'manor' – and means 'the south manor', for it lies to the south-east of Harrow. The *Town* was built up during the later part of the 19th century.

The station was opened as SUDBURY TOWN on 28 June 1903.

Swiss Cottage takes its name from a famous London public house. Here once stood an old toll gate keeper's cottage, then later a chalet. *The Swiss Tavern* was built in 1803–4, the name being changed to *Swiss Cottage* at a later date. The building was reconstructed in 1965. Built to the design of a Swiss cottage, it claims to be the largest 'pub' in London. When the railway was extended in 1868 to this part of north-west London, the name was taken for the station, and later for the district.

The Metropolitan Railway station was opened as SWISS COTTAGE on 13 April 1868 and closed as from 18 August 1940. The replacing tube station opened on 20 November 1939 on the Bakerloo Line Stanmore branch, which then became part of the Jubilee Line on 1 May 1979.

Ye Olde Swiss Cottage having its sign spruced up on a dank day at the end of the nineteenth century.

T

Temple. The site of the Law Courts and London's lawyers stands on land once owned by the Knights *Templars*, members of a military and religious Order founded in Jerusalem in about 1118. Their task was to protect the holy places and their name derives from the place where they had their quarters, near the site of Solomon's *Temple*. The name Temple was also given to their quarters in London and Paris. The Pope dissolved the Order in 1312 and the buildings have been used by the legal profession from the 14th century.

Prior to the station's opening the name Norfolk Street was considered, but it was opened as Temple on 30 May 1870.

Theydon Bois was known as *Thayden de Bosco* and held by *Hugh de Bossco* in 1240, but this family name seems to be of local and not French origin and is derived from the *wood* in *Theydon*. *Theydon* itself means, perhaps, a 'valley where thatch was obtained'.

The station was opened as Theydon by the Great Eastern Railway on 24 April 1865; re-named Theydon Bois on 1 December 1865. First used by Underground trains on 25 September 1949.

Tooting Bec. Tooting was recorded as *Totinge* in 675 and *Totinge* in the Domesday Book. From c.1082 it comprised two manors – that of *Upper Tooting* and *Tooting Bec*, held in 1086 by the Abbey of St Mary of *Bec* in Normandy and *Tooting Bec* is so named. *Tooting* is derived from a personal name of the Saxon *Tota* and

Tooting Broadway before the arrival of the Tube.

the Old English place name word ending *ing*, literally 'the people who lived at' – Tooting, therefore means – 'the home of Tota's people'. It is suggested that it should be also interpreted as 'people of the look-out place' but this is doubtful as there is no hill in Tooting.

The station was opened as TRINITY ROAD on 13 September 1926; re-named TOOTING BEC 1 October 1950.

Tooting Broadway – see Tooting Bec. The *Broadway*, once a large open space, is now a small triangular area near the station.

The station opened as TOOTING BROADWAY on 13 September 1926.

Tottenham Court Road was recorded as *Tottenheale* c.1000 and is derived from the personal name of William de *Tottenhall's* land and manor which, at the time of the Norman Conquest, belonged to the Deanery of St. Paul's Cathedral. A later name was *Toten Hall* which lay at the north-west corner of the present road. There was an ancient *court* here, much of which was demolished in 1765 to make way for the Euston Road. By the 17th century the place had become a tea garden and public amusement centre. During the early 19th century the road was built up when Bloomsbury to the east was being developed, although much was reconstructed in the early 1900s.

The Central London Railway station was opened as TOTTENHAM COURT ROAD on 30 July 1900; the adjacent Charing Cross Euston

The original Central Line entrance to Tottenham Court Road station, little changed today from this 1930s picture.

& Hampstead Railway station was opened as OXFORD STREET on 22 June 1907 and re-named TOTTENHAM COURT ROAD on 9 March 1908 (see also Goodge Street).

Tottenham Hale. Tottenham was recorded as *Toteham* in the Domesday Book and the name is derived from the personal name of the Saxon *Totta* and Old English *ham*, 'a homestead' – 'the home of Totta' and his family who once lived on a site here. *Hale* is derived from the Old English *healh*, 'a corner of land'. It was recorded as *le Hale* in 1502 and was the home of Richard atte *Hale* in 1274.

The station was opened as TOTTENHAM HALE on 1 September 1968.

Totteridge & Whetstone. *Totteridge* was recorded as *Taterugg* in 1248 and is derived from the personal name of a Saxon *Totta* and a ridge of a hill where he lived – and thus means 'Totta's ridge'. *Whetstone* was recorded as *Wheston* in 1417 and means 'the stone quarry'. Tradition holds that there was once a large stone here on which the soldiers sharpened their steel before the battle of Barnet in 1471.

The station was opened as TOTTERIDGE by the Great Northern Railway on 1 April 1872 and was re-named TOTTERIDGE & WHETSTONE on 1 April 1874. It was first used by Underground trains on 14 April 1940.

Tower Hill was recorded as *Tourhulle* in 1343 and takes its name from the nearby *Tower of London*, notorious in history as the place of public execution of the traitors taken here from the Tower. 125 people are known to have died here between 1381–1745 and a slab in nearby Trinity Square Gardens marks the scaffold site. At the foot of *Tower Hill* stands a new kiosk to that which from 1870–96 was the entrance to London's first tube tunnel under the Thames.

Prior to the station's opening the name SEETHING LANE was considered, but it was opened as MARK LANE on 6 October 1884 and re-named TOWER HILL 1 September 1946. It was re-sited on 5 February 1967 on the place where a station called TOWER OF LONDON had been in use from 25 September 1882 to 12 October 1884.

Tufnell Park was named in honour of William *Tufnell* who held the manor of Barnsbury in 1753. *Tufnell Park Road* runs to the east of the station, but there is no park in the area.

The station was opened as TUFNELL PARK on 22 June 1907.

Turnham Green was recorded as *Turneham* in c.1229 and was once a hamlet on the Great West Road. The name is derived from the Old English *turn*, 'circular' and *hamm*, 'a water meadow' – and means literally 'the bend at the river' referring to the nearby River Thames. *The Green* was first recorded in 1396 where Christ Church now stands. Incidentally, it was here, during the Civil War, that King Charles's troops were checked by the rebel Parliament's Trained Bands of Londoners.

The station, which would more accurately be named Bedford Park, was opened as TURNHAM GREEN by the London & South Western Railway on 1 January 1869 and first used by Underground trains on 1 June 1877. The rebuilt station was opened on 3 December 1911.

Turnpike Lane once belonged to the 'Stamford Hill and Green Lanes Turnpike Trust' and a *turnpike* gate was erected in 1767 at the Hornsey *Lane* (now Tottenham Lane) end of the road; it was removed in the 1870s. A '*Turnpike*' was a gate set across a road to stop those who were liable to pay a toll. Originally this was a frame consisting of two crossbars armed with *pikes* and *turning* on a *post* – hence the name.

The names DUCKETS GREEN and HARRINGAY were considered but the station was opened as TURNPIKE LANE on 19 September 1932.

U

Upminster was recorded as *Upmynstre* in 1062 and the name is derived from *mynster*, which refers to a church served by several clergy, rather than to a monastery. The prefix *up* means 'higher ground', although the town does not rise much above sixty feet. *Upminster* means – 'the church on high land'. The name of this area was originally Chafford, a corruption of St Chad's Ford and tradition asks us to believe that the brothers St Chad and St Cedd used it as one of their preaching centres when they brought Christianity to Essex in c.670.

The station was opened as UPMINSTER by the London, Tilbury & Southend Railway on 1 May 1885 and first used by Underground trains on 2 June 1902.

Upminster Bridge – see Upminster. To the right of the station, under the railway bridge and near the 'Bridge House' pub, there is a small iron road bridge, marked *Upminster Bridge*. Tradition

The trams on their long journey to Shepherd's Bush were competing more directly with the GWR service to Uxbridge than the Metropolitan Railway's extension from Harrow-on-the-Hill which opened in 1904.

has it that the Romans built a ford here over the River Ingrebourne during Cæsar's invasion of England. It seems that in c.1300 a wooden bridge was built to replace the ford. The present bridge was erected by Essex County Council in 1891.

The station was opened as UPMINSTER BRIDGE on 17 December 1934.

Upney simply means the *upper-stream* and this local natural feature gives the name to this district. Derived from Old English *upp* (higher up) and *eg* (stream).

The station was opened as UPNEY on 12 September 1932.

Upton Park. Upton is derived from *up* and Old English *tun* – a farm – and means 'the farm, or homestead on higher ground' once in a *park*, and the district is so named.

The station was opened as UPTON PARK by the L.T.S.R. in 1877 and first used by Underground trains on 2 June 1902.

Uxbridge was recorded as *Oxebruge* c.1145 and the name is derived from a 7th century tribe, the Wixan, who settled here, and in the course of time this has been abbreviated to *Ux*. The *bridge* is an ancient one over the river Colne and has variant spellings until recorded as *Uxbridge* in 1398.

The original station was opened as UXBRIDGE on 4 July 1904, and was replaced by the present re-sited station on 4 December 1938.

V

Vauxhall is named from the Norman *Falkes de Breauté* who obtained the manor of Lambeth by his marriage to the heiress Margaret de Riparus (or Redvers) in c. 1220, the manor being granted to him in 1233. Recorded as *Faukeshale* in 1279, corrupted to *Fox Hall* then eventually to *Vauxhall*.

The Undergound station opened as VAUXHALL on 23 July 1971.

Victoria. Like many other places the station was named in honour of Queen *Victoria*. The main-line station, opened on 1 October 1860, stands on piles over the basin of the former Grosvenor Canal.

The Underground station opened as VICTORIA on 24 December 1868.

Forecourt of Victoria station towards the end of the nineteenth century.

W

Walthamstow Central was recorded as *Wilcumestowe* c.1075 and the name may be derived from the Old English *wilcume*, 'welcome' and *stow*, 'a holy place' – 'the holy place with a welcome'. Alternatively the name may derive from a religious place once founded here by a woman named *Wilcume*. It was recorded as *Walthanstowe* in 1446.

The original station was opened as WALTHAMSTOW (HOE STREET) by the Great Eastern Railway on 26 April 1870; it was re-named WALTHAMSTOW CENTRAL on 6 May 1968. Underground trains ran from 1 September 1968.

Wanstead was recorded as *Waenstede* in 1066 and the name is derived from the Old English *waen*, 'waggon' and *stede*, 'place'. It seems that there was once a ford here, where waggons crossed a stream, and 'stede' usually meant a holy place - therefore *Wanstead* means 'to the holy place, near the ford crossed by waggons'.

The station was opened as WANSTEAD on 14 December 1947.

Warren Street. The estate in this area was owned by Charles Fitzroy, created Baron Southampton in 1780, who married Anne, the daughter of Sir Peter *Warren*. When the street was named in 1799 it was called *Warren Street* in her honour.

The station was opened as EUSTON ROAD on 22 June 1907 and was re-named WARREN STREET on 7 June 1908.

Warwick Avenue. Many of the streets in the old manor of Paddington are connected with families who leased land from the Bishop of London. The original lessee was Sir John Frederick of Burwood in Surrey. His great-grandson married Jane *Warwick* of Warwick Hall in Cumberland in 1778 and the street is named in her honour.

Prior to the station's opening the name was planned to have been WARRINGTON CRESCENT, but it was opened as WARWICK AVENUE on 31 January 1915.

Waterloo was named in commemoration of the Battle of *Waterloo* (1815). The name was also given to the new bridge over the River Thames (originally called Strand Bridge) which was opened by the Prince Regent on 18 June 1817, the second anniversary of the Battle. The name was adopted for the main-line station opened on 11 July 1848, and later for the locality.

The Waterloo & City Line was built and run by the London & South Western Railway and its station was opened as WATERLOO on 8 August 1898. Ownership of the line and stations was transferred to London Underground on 5 April 1994. The Bakerloo Line station was opened as WATERLOO on 10 March 1906, followed by the Northern Line station on 13 August 1926.

Watford was recorded in 944 and the name is derived from the Old English *waed*, 'place for wading' or *wad*, 'hunting' – and means 'ford which is used by hunters', from a once nearby natural feature.

The station was opened as WATFORD on 2 November 1925.

The centre of Watford in the early 1930s.

Wembley Central was recorded as *Wemba lea* in 825 and the name is derived from the personal name *Wemba* and the Old English *leah*, 'forest clearing' – and means 'the clearing where Wemba lived'. This name may be a nickname or could be taken from *Wemba*, the name of a Gothic King. It has had various spellings until recorded as *Wembley* in 1535.

A station called SUDBURY was opened by the London & Birmingham Railway in 1842. It was re-named SUDBURY & WEMBLEY on 1 May 1882 and WEMBLEY FOR SUDBURY on 1 November 1910. The present station was first used for Underground trains as WEMBLEY FOR SUDBURY on 16 April 1917; re-named WEMBLEY CENTRAL 5 July 1948.

Wembley Park – see Wembley Central. The Wembley stadium, exhibition and entertainment complex occupies the area of the original park.

The station was opened as WEMBLEY PARK on 12 May 1894.

West Acton – see Acton Town.

The station was opened as WEST ACTON on 5 November 1923.

Westbourne Park was recorded as *Westburn* in 1222 and is derived from the Old English *westan* and *burnam*, 'place'- means 'the place west of the stream'. Paddington was the sister village on the east bank. The road here was an ancient lane winding through the old *Westbourne Farm*. The Green was recorded in 1680 hence the *Park*, now a road.

The station was opened as WESTBOURNE PARK on 1 February 1866.

West Brompton signifies *Broom Town* with suggestions of a wide common – and means 'the common with the broom trees, near a town'.

Prior to the station's opening the name RICHMOND ROAD was planned, reflecting the name of this part of Old Brompton Road which lasted into the 1920s. It was opened as WEST BROMPTON on 12 April 1869.

The original station building at West Brompton, seen here about 1910, is still recognisable today.

West Finchley – see Finchley Central.

The station was opened as WEST FINCHLEY by the London & North Eastern Railway on 1 March 1933 and first used by Underground trains on 14 April 1940.

West Ham was recorded as *Hamme* in 958 which signifies that this and *East Ham* were then only one geographical location and it was not until 1186 that the name *Westhamma* was recorded. The name is derived from the Old English *hamm*, 'a water meadow '- referring to the low-lying riverside meadow near the bend of the Thames. (See also East Ham.)

The station was opened as WEST HAM by the London Tilbury & Southend Railway on 1 February 1901 and was first used by Underground trains on 2 June 1902.

West Hampstead – see Hampstead.
    The station was opened as West Hampstead on 30 June 1879.

West Harrow – see Harrow-on-the-Hill.
    The station opened as West Harrow on 17 November 1913.

West Kensington – see Kensington.
    The station opened as North End (Fulham) on 9 September 1874; re-named West Kensington 1 March 1877.

Westminster. By tradition the site of the Abbey was first known as Torneia (785) and means 'thorn island', being once a low lying islet regularly cut off from the mainland at high tide. Recorded as *Westminster* in 785, the name is derived from west and Old English *mynster*, 'monastery' or 'church', the west because it lies to the west of London. *Westminster Abbey* began as a small church attached to a Benedictine monastery, was rebuilt in the eleventh century and completed in 1388. The village of *Westminster* (a City since 1540) was joined up to London in the 18th century.
    The station opened as Westminster Bridge on 24 December 1868; re-named Westminster 1907.

West Ruislip – see Ruislip.
    The adjacent main line station was opened by the Great Western & Great Central Joint Committee on 2 April 1906 as Ruislip & Ickenham. It was re-named West Ruislip on 30 June 1947. In preparation for the opening of the Underground station, the committee of the New Works Programme 1935/40 suggested naming it Ickenham Green. However, delayed by the Second World War, the Underground station was opened as West Ruislip on 21 November 1948.

Whitechapel takes its name from the *white* stone *chapel* of St Mary Matfelon, first built in 1329, then rebuilt three times, until bombed in 1940 and finally demolished in 1952. Today there is no trace of the church that gave its name to this district.
    The station was opened as Whitechapel on 10 April 1876; first used by Underground trains 1 October 1884.

White City. The sports stadium was opened in 1908 to house part of the Franco-British Exhibition. The strikingly white finish of the buildings, and the exhibits in the main hall (all of which were white), earned the stadium its name.
    The Hammersmith & City Line station was opened on 1 May 1908, and the Central Line station on 14 May 1908, both as

Wood Lane. The Central Line station was re-sited and both re-named White City 23 November 1947. The Hammersmith & City station was closed from 25 October 1959; since 1 November 1914 it had been used only on special occasions.

Willesden Green was recorded as *Willesdone Grene* in 1254 and was formerly a distinct hamlet. *Willesden* itself was recorded as *Willesdune* in 939 and is derived from the Old English *wiell*, 'spring' and *dun*, 'hill', and means – hill of the spring', referring to a once nearby natural location. *Willesden* was the name adopted c.1840 by the London & Birmingham Railway from the earlier spelling of *Wilsdon*.

The station was opened as Willesden Green on 24 November 1879.

Willesden Junction – see Willesden Green. The name has its origin in the railway *junction* at this point.

The station was opened as Willesden Junction by the London & North Western Railway on 1 September 1866 and was first used by Underground trains on 10 May 1915.

Wimbledon was recorded as *Wunemannedunne* c.950 and is derived from the personal name of the Saxon *Winebeald* and *down*, 'a hill' – means 'the hill where Winebeald lived', with his family. It has had various spellings in the course of time until recorded as *Wimbledon* in 1211.

The original London & Southampton Railway station opened as Wimbledon on 21 May 1838. The platforms for terminating District Line trains were opened on 3 June 1889.

The Southern Railway's architectural design arguably ran a close second to that of the Underground. This is Wimbledon, terminus of the District line from Earl's Court and seen in the 1950s.

Wimbledon Park – see Wimbledon. The Park is to the west of the station.

The station was opened as WIMBLEDON PARK by the London & South Western Railway for the use of their own and District Railway trains on 3 June 1889.

Woodford, as the name suggests, means 'the ford by a wood', over the River Roding which runs through the district.

The station was opened as WOODFORD by the Eastern Counties Railway on 22 August 1856 and first used by Underground trains on 14 December 1947.

Wood Green was recorded as *Wodegrene* in 1502 and was once a separate hamlet on the edge of Enfield Chase. As the name suggests it means 'the wood by the green'.

Prior to the station's opening the name LORDSHIP LANE was proposed, but it was opened as WOOD GREEN on 19 September 1932.

Wood Lane. There have been three stations in the area with this name, the latest being a new station on the Hammersmith & City line. The other two were a station on the same line situated across the road from the present one, closer to Shepherd's Bush, opened 1 May 1908 and closed 25 October 1959 (by which time it had been renamed White City) and a terminal station on the Central London Railway opened 14 May 1908 and closed 23 November 1947 (to be replaced by the Central Line station named White City further to the north). The name Wood Lane came into use here in the first few decades of the 19th century and reflects the fact that this was once situated in London's countryside. It is one of nine Wood Lanes in Greater London, but with the presence of the BBC Television Centre and the new Underground station serving the Westfield development, this is undoubtedly the best known of them.

The present Wood Lane station opened on 13 October 2008.

Woodside Park was recorded as *Fyncheley Wode* in 1468 and was part of the great Middlesex woodland area. It was named *Woodside* in 1686 – being at the side of the wood.

The station was opened as TORRINGTON PARK, WOODSIDE by the Great Northern Railway on 1 April 1872. It was re-named WOODSIDE PARK on 1 May 1882 and was first used by Underground trains on 14 April 1940.

Stations on Docklands Light Rail

All Saints is the name of the nearby church which was designed by Charles Hollis and was consecrated in 1823. Until 1817 this was the name of one of parishes of London.

The station was opened on 31 August 1987.

Bank – see Bank Underground.

The DLR station was opened on 29 July 1991.

Beckton was named in 1869 in honour of a Mr S.A. Beck, the then Governor of the local Gas Light & Coke Company.

The station was opened on 28 March 1994.

Beckton Park – see Beckton. To the north of the station are the two parks which the station is named after – 'South Beckton District Park' and 'New Beckton Park'.

The station was opened on 28 March 1994.

Blackwall appears in records as *Blackvale* as early as 1337, and sometimes as *Bleak wall*, possibly from Old English *blaee* and maybe refers to a windy stretch of the River Thames. The shipyard was built in the late 16th century and contained the original entrance to the West India Docks.

The station was opened on 28 March 1994.

Bow Church – see Bow Road Underground. To the right of the station, in the main Bow Road, there is a traffic island on which stands Bow Church. Its full name is 'Saint Mary Bow Church', the site of which has been a place of worship since the 14th century.

The station was opened on 31 August 1987.

Canary Wharf – see page 14

Canning Town – see page 15

Crossharbour is a new development which was placed at the crossing of Glengall Grove. The name is appropriate for it is in the centre of the Isle of Dogs.

The station opened as CROSSHARBOUR on 13 August 1987 and re-named CROSSHARBOUR & LONDON ARENA in 1994 and back to plain CROSSHARBOUR in 2007 following demolition of the Arena.

Custom House takes its name from the building which once stood at the north side of the Victoria Docks and today still gives its name to a district in this part of London. The area was developed as a working class residential working district from the 1880s onwards.

The station was opened in 1885 as Victoria Dock on the North Woolwich Railway. When the line was re-developed in the 1980s the station's name was changed to Custom House. The adjacent DLR station opened on 28 March 1994.

Cutty Sark is the name, of course, of the famous sailing ship, now preserved near the station in dry dock. This is one of the few surviving tea clippers of the nineteenth century. Built at Dumbarton, Scotland (in 1869) she was engaged on the China tea trade. Later, on the Australian grain run, she achieved a new sailing record of 73 days for the London–Sydney passage.

The station was opened on 20 November 1999.

Cyprus. This small area to the north side of the Royal Albert Dock takes its name from the island of Cyprus, for the original owners traded mainly with this island at the eastern end of the Mediterranean Sea.

The station was opened on 28 March 1994.

Deptford Bridge. Deptford was recorded as *Depeford* in 1293 and the name is self explanatory from the Old English *deop* and *ford* - means the 'Deep ford', from the location of the land. The bridge crosses the Ravensbourne River and maybe the Romans built a bridge here, which was later destroyed by the Danes. A wooden bridge was built here in the 14th century and was replaced by a stone bridge in 1809.

The station was opened on 20 November 1999.

Devons Road was known as Bromley Lane c.1790 and it seems that it was named after a Thomas *Devon* who once owned land in this area or maybe one of his ancestors, for his household was listed at one time in the local 'poor rate' records.

The station was opened on 31 August 1987.

East India takes its name from the 'East India Company' founded as early as 1600. The company obtained an Act of Parliament in 1803 for the docks to be built, which were ready for use in 1806. As the name suggests the Company traded on the routes to India and the Far East and the 'Cutty Sark' was one of the original clippers.

The station was opened on 28 March 1994.

Elverson Road. Little is known about how this road obtained its name; one must presume that it was named after a local landowner when the road was built between 1875 and 1893.

The station was opened on 20 November 1999.

Gallions Reach takes it name from a former hotel built in this area in 1803 for the use of passengers embarking from the adjacent jetty. The word 'Reach' means a straight portion of a river (the nearby River Thames).

The station was opened on 28 November 1994.

Greenwich – see North Greenwich Underground.

The station was opened on 20 November 1999. It is adjacent to the original terminus of the London & Greenwich Railway.

Heron Quays. Unlike Canary Wharf, this is one of the places in London whose name really means what is stated, for the Quay takes its name from the herons which at one time nested on the old buildings in this area, and maybe on a good day they can still be seen. All this was noted in the local *City of London Recorder* in 1987. A *quay* is a landing place for the loading and unloading of ships (from the Old French *quai* – an enclosure).

The station was opened on 31 August 1987.

Island Gardens. In 1895 a formal garden was laid out here by the London County Council on former waste land. Initially the park was called the Island Garden.

The station was opened on 31 August 1987.

King George V. The station is named after the nearby docks, in turn named after the reigning monarch at the time the building of the docks, by the Port of London Authority, began in 1912. Construction was delayed by the First World War and they opened in 1921.

The station opened on 6 December 2005.

Langdon Park. The station carries the name of the nearby park that opened in 1963. The park and a local school are named after the Reverend C. G. Langdon, vicar of All Angels, Bromley-by-Bow between 1913 and 1925, for his work among the poor.

The station opened on 9 December 2007.

Lewisham was recorded as *Levesham* in the Domesday Book and the name is derived from the personal name of the Saxon *Leofsa* and the Old English *tun* 'a homestead'. The name changed to its present spelling in the course of time.

The station was opened on 20 November 1999.

Limehouse was recorded as *Le Lymhostes* in 1367 and means 'The *oasts* or *kilns*' from the Old English *lim* and *ast*. Therefore the place name really means what the word suggests.

The station was opened on 31 August 1987.

London City Airport is named after the airport opened in 1987 for short take-off and landing aircraft.

The station opened on 6 December 2005.

Mudchute. The Mudchute is the adjacent hill of mud dredged from the Millwall dock over the years – hence this rather unusual name.

The station was opened on 31 August 1987 and re-sited for the Lewisham extension which opened on 20 November 1999.

Pontoon Dock. The word pontoon is from the French *ponton* which means a bridge.

The station opened on 6 December 2005.

Poplar was recorded as '*Poplar*' in 1327 and means the (Place at) the *poplar tree*', probably a local meeting point in ancient times.

The station was opened on 31 August 1987.

Prince Regent is a small area of the London docks which was built in the 1880s. It was named in memory of the Prince Regent (1762–1830) who later became George IV.

The station was opened on 28 March 1994.

Pudding Mill Lane. Very little is recorded of this place name, but we can presume that the meaning is similar to Pudding Lane in the City of London. It seems that butchers had their scalding houses here as early as the 12th century and it is suggested that 'puddings' was the nickname for butcher's offal. The Mill was once nearby.

The station was opened in February 1996.

Royal Albert. In 1875 Act of Parliament was obtained to construct the Royal Albert Docks, which were completed by 1880. They were opened by the then Duke of Connaught and were named in honour of Prince Albert (1819–1861) the Prince Consort of Queen Victoria.

The station was opened on 28 March 1994.

Royal Victoria was the name of the docks which were constructed between 1850 and 1855 being named in honour of Queen Victoria. The 'Royal' part of the name was added in 1880 and the docks were rebuilt between 1935 and 1944.

The station was opened on 28 March 1994.

Shadwell was recorded as *Scadeuuelle* in Domesday Book and as *Shadewell* in 1233 and means – a 'shallow well' from a once nearby local spring.

The DLR station opened on 31 August 1987.

South Quay is now a business and residential area on the Isle of Dogs. It is located to the south of the West India Docks hence its name. A *Quay* is a landing place for the loading and unloading of ships (from the Old French *quai* – an enclosure).

The station was opened on 31 August 1987.

Stratford – see page 65.

The DLR station opened on 31 August 1987.

Tower Gateway, as the name suggests, is the 'Gateway' into the Tower of London (see Tower Hill Underground for further information and history).

The station was opened on 31 August 1987.

Westferry. The name is self-explanatory and is close to the West India Docks. Ferry means to transport from one place to another (from Old English *ferian* – to carry).

The station was opened on 31 August 1987.

West India Quay. The area covered by the 'West India' docks comprised the largest of the original enclosed docks in the Port of London. They were built between 1802 and 1806 and cover part of the area known as the Isle of Dogs. Built originally for a 21 year monopoly of trade with the West Indies, they were later used also for India and Far East. It was not built by a shipping company, unlike the East India Docks. A *Quay* is a landing place for loading and unloading ships (from the Old French *quai* – an enclosure).

The station was opened on 31 August 1987.

West Silvertown is an industrial and residential district south of the Royal Victoria Docks. It was developed in the 1850s around the rubber and telegraph works of S.W. Silver and Company – hence the name Silvertown.

The station opened on 6 December 2005.

Woolwich Arsenal is named after the Thames-side town's armaments factory that closed in 1967. The derivation of the name Woolwich is uncertain, though as with Greenwich the second syllable of the name comes from the Old English *wic* meaning village (usually one located adjacent to water). The Wool part of the name may simply indicate that the village was a trading centre for wool.

The station opened on 10 January 2009.

Bibliography

F. R. Banks: **The Penguin Guide to London**, Penguin Books, 1973

Gillian Bebbington: **London Street Names**, B. T. Batsford Ltd, London, 1972.

John Bromley: **The Armorial Bearings of the Guilds of London**, Frederick Warne & Co. Ltd, London, 1960.

Kenneth Cameron: **English Place Names**, B. T. Batsford Ltd, London, 1961.

Harold P. Clunn: **The Face of London**, Simkin Marshall Ltd, London, 1932.

Basil E. Cracknell: **Portrait of London River**, Robert Hale Ltd, London, 1968.

G.J. Copley: **English Place Names and their Origins**, David & Charles, Newton Abbot, 1968.

Eilert Ekwall: **The Concise Oxford Dictionary of English Place Names**, Oxford University Press, 1960.

Eilert Ekwall: **Street-Names of the City of London**, Oxford University Press, London, 1965.

Geoffrey Evans: **Kensington**, Hamish Hamilton, London, 1975.

Charles James Féret: **Fulham Old and New** (Vol. 1), Simpkin Marshall Hamilton Kent & Co. Ltd, London, 1900.

John Field: **Discovering Place-Names**. Shire Publications, Tring, 1971.

Margaret Gellings, W. F. H. Nicolaisen and Melville Richards: **The Names of Towns and Cities in Britain**, B. T. Batsford Ltd, London, 1970.

Edward Gordon and A.F.C. Deeson: **The Book of Bloomsbury**, Edward Gordon (Arts) Ltd, London, 1950

J.E.B. Gover, A. Mawer and F.M. Stenton: **The Place Names of Surrey**, Cambridge University Press, 1934.

Henry A. Harben: **A Dictionary of London**, Herbert Jenkins Ltd, London, 1918.

J. Edward Hart: **London Oddities**, London Transport, London, 1974.

Godfrey James: **London and the Western Reaches**, Robert Hale Ltd, London, 1950.

William Kent: **An Encyclopaedia of London**, J. M. Dent & Sons Ltd, London, 1970.

A. Mawer and F. M. Stenton: **The Place Names of Middlesex**, Cambridge University Press, 1942.

A. Mawer and F. M. Stenton: **The Place Names of Hertfordshire**, Cambridge University Press, 1938.

Arthur Mee: **The King's England – Essex**, Hodder & Stoughton, London, 1966.

Arthur Mee: **The King's England – London North of the Thames**, Hodder & Stoughton, London, 1972.

W. G. Moore: **The Penguin Encyclopaedia of Places**, Penguin Books, Middlesex, 1971.

Douglas Newton: **London West of the Bars**, Robert Hale Ltd, London, 1951

Nicholson's: **Footloose in London**, Robert Nicholson Publications, London.

André Page: **What you should know about London**, Midas Books, Tunbridge Wells, Kent, 1973.

P. H. Reaney: **The Place-Names of Essex**, Cambridge University Press, 1935.

P. H. Reaney: **The Origin of English Place-Names**, Routledge & Kegan Paul, London, 1961.

Michael Robbins: **Middlesex**, Collins, London, 1953.

Douglas Rose: **The London Underground – A Diagrammatic History**, Douglas Rose 1999.

Gordon Ross: **A History of County Cricket, Surrey**, Arthur Barker Ltd, London, 1971.

Stuart Rossiter: **The Blue Guides – London**, Ernest Benn, Ltd, Kent, 1973.

Lilian and Ashmore Russan: **Historic Streets of London**, Simpkin Marshall Hamilton Kent & Co. Ltd, London, 1923.

A.I. Smith: **Dictionary of City of London Street Names**, David & Charles, Newton Abbot, 1970.

H.G. Stokes: **English Place-Names**, B. T. Batsford Ltd, London, 1949.

Bruce Stevenson: **Middlesex**, B. T. Batsford Ltd, London, 1972.

Ben Weinreb and Christopher Hibbert: **The London Encyclopaedia**, 1983.

Cuthbert Wilfrid Whitaker: **History of Enfield** (1911), Enfield Preservation Society, reprint, 1969.

Guy R. Williams: **London in the Country**, Hamish Hamilton, London, 1975.

Leonard F. Wise: **World Rulers**, Ward Lock Educational, Sterling Publishing Co. Inc., 1967.

John Wittich: **Discovering London Curiosities**, Shire Publications Ltd, Aylesbury, 1973.

Pieter Zwart: **Islington: A History and Guide**, Sidgwick & Jackson, London, 1973.